WHAT IT'S LIKE

5/26/16

To Joel,

Dream BIG!

—JB

to Climb Mount Everest, Blast Off into Space, Survive a Tornado, and Other Extraordinary Stories

by Jeff Belanger

For my daughter, Sophie.
You can achieve anything you believe in.
—J.B.

STERLING and the distinctive Sterling logo are registered trademarks of
Sterling Publishing Co., Inc.

Library of Congress Cataloging-in-Publication Data

Belanger, Jeff.
What it's like-- / Jeff Belanger.
p. cm.
Includes index.
ISBN 978-1-4027-6711-1
1. Courage--Anecdotes--Juvenile literature. I. Title.
BJ1533.C8B45 2010
179'.6--dc22

2009040875

Lot#:
2 4 6 8 10 9 7 5 3 1
10/10
Published by Sterling Publishing Co., Inc.
387 Park Avenue South, New York, NY 10016
© 2011 by Jeff Belanger
Distributed in Canada by Sterling Publishing
c/o Canadian Manda Group, 165 Dufferin Street
Toronto, Ontario, Canada M6K 3H6
Distributed in the United Kingdom by GMC Distribution Services
Castle Place, 166 High Street, Lewes, East Sussex, England BN7 1XU
Distributed in Australia by Capricorn Link (Australia) Pty. Ltd.
P.O. Box 704, Windsor, NSW 2756, Australia

Sterling ISBN 978-1-4027-6711-1

For information about custom editions, special sales, premium and
corporate purchases, please contact Sterling Special Sales
Department at 800-805-5489 or specialsales@sterlingpublishing.com.

WHAT IT'S LIKE

to Climb Mount Everest,
Blast Off into Space,
Survive a Tornado,
and Other
Extraordinary Stories

by Jeff Belanger

STERLING

New York / London
www.sterlingpublishing.com/kids

WHAT IT'S LIKE ...
To Read This Book

Have you ever heard a story about a person who survived a horrible accident, or who accomplished a feat so big that you couldn't believe a human being was capable of such a thing? We sometimes think these people are superheroes when we hear about their ordeals in the news. They're not.

You're about to meet twelve individuals who are just like you. Some of these folks made a decision to work toward something big, and never gave up until they reached their goal. Others didn't intend to end up in a terrible situation, but when they found themselves in great danger, they rose above the challenge and did what was necessary to survive.

Anything can be accomplished if you set your mind and heart on the goal. You can fly into space, race across the sky, climb the highest mountain, survive horrible storms, and come out better for it. These twelve people have learned for themselves that they're strong, smart, and capable. Though they didn't set out to inspire others, they do. Their stories are moving, and make us wonder what greatness is waiting out there for us.

Sit down and meet twelve ordinary people who have done extraordinary things.

YOU'RE ABOUT TO FIND OUT WHAT IT'S LIKE . . .

WHAT IT'S LIKE . . .

To Be Attacked by a Shark

NAME: Bethany Hamilton
DATE: October 31, 2003
LOCATION: North Shore,
Kauai, Hawaii

I t's early morning—still dark—when I head out on the water with my best friend, Alana, her brother, Byron, and her dad, Holt. I don't ever surf alone because it's not safe. We paddle out about a mile. The waves are just kiddie waves, so Alana and I play and goof around while Byron and Holt look for waves to catch a short distance away. After a few minutes, I decide to lie on my stomach on my board and wait for the waves to pick up. I'm still in sight of the others. My left arm is dangling in the water.

Then I notice this gray blur glide by and sort of grab hold of my left arm. I feel a back-and-forth tug. I hold on to my board with my legs and right arm. I don't hear any noise in the water, and I don't feel a change of current. I just see the gray blur, and then it disappears. I look down and see my arm is gone! The water is red with my blood. My body must be in shock because I don't feel any pain. I realize a shark just tore off my arm. I scream out to Alana and her family, "I've been bitten by a shark!"

A chunk of my surfboard is gone. The shark bit right through it. At first, Alana and Holt don't believe me, but they quickly see the blood. They see that my arm is gone. I'm not crying because it still doesn't hurt. It's just numb and I can't believe what's happened.

"I've been bitten by a shark!"

The others swim over to me immediately. Holt ties his surfboard leash around my shoulder. This acts as a tourniquet, cutting off the flow of blood so I don't bleed to death. I don't look down. I can't. I mean, I know my arm is missing, and I know it's bad. I'm scared to look. I'm still losing blood. So many thoughts are going through my mind, but—as weird as it sounds—I'm worrying about losing my surfing sponsor. I worry about participating in surfing competitions again.

"Get into shore, get into shore," I quietly say to myself over and over. Holt tells me to stay awake and keep talking, so I just pray to God to rescue me, to send help. I hold on to my board. Holt sends Byron to shore to call for an ambulance. He paddles back quickly. Holt pulls me to the beach as fast as he can, but the swim takes almost fifteen minutes because we're so far out. I still don't feel any pain. It's just numb and cold around my shoulder.

We finally reach the beach. I feel really tired and I just want to go to sleep, but Holt is yelling at me to stay awake. I know I'm losing a lot of blood and I know it's possible I could die. I just pray and pray. I'm scared, but I have faith that God will protect me.

There's only one major road in Kauai, and the hospital is forty-five minutes away by car. The ambulance ride is long and we drive past beach shacks, on dirt roads, and over one-lane bridges. The driver is speeding to the hospital. I feel the bumps in the road. I listen to what the paramedics say to me. I'm thirsty and sleepy, but I say prayers to keep myself from passing out on the long ride to the hospital. The paramedics and doctors won't give me anything to drink because I'm about to go through major surgery. By the time I reach the operating room, I've lost 60 percent of my blood. . . .

I wake up in my hospital bed and learn that I'm going to be okay. During the surgery, the doctors were able to stop the bleeding and fill the wound with gauze to keep it clean. I'll have to go through a couple of rounds of surgery to make sure there's no infection. The plan is to keep the wound covered but open for a few days to constantly clean it, then doctors will sew the skin shut. So I spend the next week in the hospital.

In the hospital, I'm bored. I want to get back out and surf again. My family is relieved that I'm alive. They can't seem to understand that my priority is to get back in the water. Alana also seems shaken by seeing me without an arm, but I know she understands my desire to surf again. I can't believe how many people send flowers. There are reporters who want to talk to me about what happened.

The shark experts can't figure out why I was attacked. Sharks rarely go after people and aren't usually found in water that shallow. Everyone is treating me like a celebrity. But I just want to go surf again.

I learn that I was bitten by a fourteen-foot tiger shark that weighed about one ton. People can only guess why it chose me. Maybe it thought I looked like a sea turtle. Some people think something was wrong with the shark. I won't ever know.

Finally, after a full week in the hospital, I'm allowed to go home.

Adjusting to life with only one arm is tough. Getting dressed is different. I start to figure out little tricks—like how to peel an orange with only one hand. I sometimes look at other girls on the beach with their perfect bodies and feel a little self-conscious. But I'm healthy. I've survived a shark attack. And now I have a sense that everyone is beautiful in their own unique way—including me.

I want to get right back in the water because surfing is in my blood. Giving it up was never an option for me. The doctors tell me I have to wait three more weeks because my stitches might get infected.

It's the day before Thanksgiving, 2003. It's been twenty-six days since my shark attack, and I'm ready to get back in the water. I've been exercising to build up my strength again, and I feel good. I'm a little nervous, though. I've had plenty of nightmares about sharks since the attack. But I work every day to keep a positive and strong attitude. I know the only way to overcome the fear is to just get back out there and see how it goes. I have to try not to let my fear grab hold of me.

Swimming out with only one arm takes longer. I also spend extra time looking at my surroundings. I'm afraid of what might be in the water, but I'm more afraid of never surfing again. I'm using a longboard, which I don't like,

but every new surfer has to learn on a longboard. My shortboard allowed me to carve the waves and be more agile on the water, but I need to relearn the sport with only one arm, so I'm using the longboard. It's like I'm new to surfing again.

I see a good wave that I'd like to try, but I'm not able to get up on the board. I was so used to having both arms to pull myself up. With only one arm, I need to shift my weight differently. Another wave comes and again I can't get up. I'm frustrated. I'm afraid that I won't be as good as I was before, but I know I can find a way to surf again. When the third wave comes, I pop up on my board and stay up. I'm surfing again! I cry tears of happiness as I ride the wave all the way back to the shore.

Two years later I'm competing in the 2005 National Scholastic Surfing Association championships. I'm surfing in the Explorer women's division. It takes me a little longer to get out in the ocean, and I have to take more time to choose my specific wave. I can't afford to waste the extra time that it would take to try a wave that isn't great. I don't get or want extra time from the judges. No special treatment for me—I want to be judged the same as my competitors. I swim out with all of the other surfers. . . .

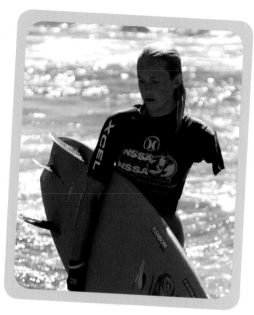

Finally I see the one I want. I stand up on my board and I'm carving through the wave. I just know it's a good one. My ride is going great. I speed through the tunnel created by the breaking of the wave, ride through the base, and have an incredible run. Sometimes you just know when you nail it.

Everyone has their day to shine, and today is my day. The judges announce the scores and I find out I took first place. My family and friends are all there to see me win my first national championship title. They have all been so supportive of me that this is like their victory, too. It's the best feeling in the world. I'm so happy to still be able to do what I love.

BETHANY HAMILTON still competes in and wins surfing competitions all over the world. In addition to being a world-famous surfer, she is also an active public speaker, author, and charity worker.

WHAT IT'S LIKE . . .
To Experience Combat

NAME: Michael Anthony
DATE: October 10, 2006
LOCATION: Mosul, Iraq

Half of my unit—about two hundred soldiers—is flying in to our base in Mosul in northern Iraq. We're in a C-1 plane that looks just like a commercial airliner, but stripped of everything. Inside, on each side of the plane, are fold-down seats. The seats fold down so that two soldiers can sit facing each other, with their equipment in the middle. There's no overhead bins, no carpet—just drab metal. We're all wearing full combat gear: a bulletproof vest that weighs about thirty pounds, a Kevlar helmet, and a rucksack, which is an oversized military backpack full of supplies, clothes, and maybe some personal items. The rucksack weighs between fifty and sixty pounds. We

An evening medical evacuation run

carry our rifles in our hands. Altogether, I'm carrying close to one hundred pounds of gear. It's mid-morning and we're about to make a combat landing because the area is "hot," which means there is active combat in the region on a regular basis. This means the plane has to go down really fast as it's approaching the runway so that it's not an easy target for the enemy.

I spent the four previous months in training at Fort McCoy in Wisconsin, so I should be reviewing what I've learned. But as we come in to land, my mind is just totally blank. From the air, the base looks like dozens of sand-colored blocks neatly placed in the desert. The plane stops, the door opens, and I concentrate on grabbing my gear and running behind the cement barriers located just off to the side of the runway at the base. Once I'm on the ground, I can see that only one or two of the many buildings are taller than one story. The buildings really blend in, which is their purpose.

I'm part of the new hospital crew that's coming in. Today everyone feels a little superstitious, because every time a new hospital crew has come to the base, it was attacked soon after. The next afternoon we run a drill: a fake "mass casualty," or a large attack where many people are injured. Dozens of other soldiers swarm into the hospital to simulate what would happen in an attack. The hospital crew practices sorting people into three categories: those who

would need immediate medical help, those who could wait, and those who wouldn't make it. This is our introduction to Iraq and to our new hospital post. After the drill, our group is now in charge of the hospital. My job is Operating Specialist. I assist the doctors in surgery. I am supposed to do whatever they need me to do—hand them instruments as they ask for them, help stitch up wounds after surgery, and hold tools when needed.

Night falls on our second day, and it's still quiet. A few of my buddies and I go to the gym. I'm working out when suddenly I hear these booming noises.

There are a few loud bangs. It's only my second day here, so I don't know what the noises are. Maybe someone is banging on some machinery nearby, or maybe a dump truck dropped a Dumpster. Then I see everyone in the gym flee out the doors, and I know we are under attack. My buddies and I drop everything and start running for the bunkers, which are large cement buildings built solidly into the ground. Besides the hospital, a bunker is the only safe place to be during an attack. The thick cement can handle direct hits from the falling bombs.

The bunkers aren't too far from the gym, but far enough that we need to make a run for it. Bombs are hitting right by the bunkers, but we have to run toward them anyway, since being in a bunker is safer than being in the gym. The bombs sound like glass doors slamming shut

Bombs are hitting right by the bunkers, but we have to run toward them anyway . . .

and shattering. Shrapnel—chunks of sharp metal that fly out from the bombs—and debris are flying all over the place. The air is becoming thick with dirt, sand, and other rubble kicked up by the explosions. I can't help but breathe it in.

I dive into the bunker and try to settle down. I've trained for this, but I realize training can take me only so far. I have to try to have confidence in my fellow soldiers, my buddies. For me, the real thought process starts once

Mosul, Iraq

I am in that bunker. Before that point, I was just acting and reacting, in the middle of the action. I only had time to think, *What is everyone else doing? Run to the bunker!*

All the other soldiers in the bunker are totally composed. Everyone— besides my two friends and me, who are part of the unit that arrived yesterday— looks like they're having a day at the beach. I'm thinking, *How can these people be so calm right now?* I've just jumped for safety into the bunker, and I yell at my buddies, "Get in here! Get in here!" But the others just kind of stroll in like this is an everyday thing. I try not to act too afraid, but I can't help it. My mind is racing. I'm asking tons of questions, pacing back and forth, and sweating. The others are just hanging out on the other side of the bunker, laughing, and telling jokes. Then I realize this *is* an everyday thing for them. This is a life-and-death situation and these people have already accepted it.

The attack goes on for another ten to fifteen minutes. I think about all of the newspaper reports I read before I came over here of attacks on American bases in Iraq and Afghanistan. Now I get it. In a day or two, someone else is going to be reading about this attack back home, and it won't mean much to them. But I'm living it. Bombs rain down at varying times. Finally, the bombs stop and it's quiet. We still need to stay in the bunker until the infantry soldiers check the area and let everyone know all is clear.

Someone in the bunker receives the radio call "All clear." We're free to go back outside. Some people start heading back to the gym, but my buddies and I need to report to the hospital right away in case there are any injuries. It's about a mile and a half away, but as we start walking back, we notice that no one else is outside. This is strange. I'm wondering what's going on. We keep on walking. We're about a quarter of a mile away from the hospital, and still no one is outside.

Finally we see a Humvee, a large military vehicle, barreling down the road toward us until it stops right next to us. The weird feeling I had earlier starts to turn into alarm. I don't know what's going on and I don't know where

we're supposed to be. One of the soldiers inside the vehicle says, "What are you doing out? The base hasn't been cleared yet—find a bunker!" Then they speed off. We look around but there are no bunkers close by. Toward the right is just a huge parking lot for Humvees, and to the left are just regular buildings. We could be in deep trouble. So we run as fast as possible toward the hospital. Just as we get inside the hospital doors, the bombs start dropping again and another attack starts. I can't believe it—we could have just been killed.

We're inside the hospital and all these casualties start coming in, just like in the drill earlier today. The first soldiers rush into the hospital. There are eight of them. Their wounds vary from shrapnel cuts to broken bones.

As an Operating Specialist, my job is to assist the doctors as efficiently as possible. One woman's injury is serious; she's a nurse, one of the hospital unit members that my group is replacing. She's been here a year and is scheduled to go home next week. Though it looks bad, she will survive and be sent home.

As I work on some of the soldiers with minor injuries, my training finally comes into use. I don't think about much except to anticipate what instrument the doctor will need next. Every time I can help the doctor, it saves blood, resources, and time. The sight of blood never bothered me, but some of the other people in my unit are freaking out. Their attitude is not helping our situation, and a doctor has to ask one person to leave.

Between operations I clean the operating room which needs to be mopped up before the next patient can be wheeled in. I move as quickly as I can. There's not much time to think, because there's always someone else who needs help.

When it's all over and I'm finally back in my bunk, I think again about the newspaper reports I used to read about the attacks on our soldiers. The press only reports the numbers, and numbers don't reflect human lives. I see the faces behind the numbers. But I am also able to help save some of those people.

The next day I walk back to the gym and dining facility, and I go past the spot where the soldiers stopped us. The parking lot full of Humvees was completely hit with bombs. Tires are blown out and there are huge craters in the pavement—in the exact spot we were standing the night before. Had we taken cover in that parking lot instead of running to the hospital, I may not have been able to tell anyone of my experience. It's only my third day in Iraq, and I already understand what war is about. With at least a year to go before it's my turn to leave, I try to focus on my job, on helping people, and on making sure I get home. A year can be a very long time.

MICHAEL ANTHONY finished his first tour in Iraq in October 2007. He wrote a book called *Mass Casualties: A Young Medic's True Story of Death, Deception, and Dishonor in Iraq* about his experience in the military. He is now living back at home in Massachusetts.

WHAT IT'S LIKE . . .
To Save People from a Burning Building

NAME: Lieutenant Jeff Kraft
DATE: April 15, 2005
LOCATION: Calumet Park, Illinois

I t's about ten o'clock at night. There are only three of us on duty for the Calumet Park Fire Department: an engineer, myself, and one other firefighter. It's a little stressful because it's the first day on the job for one of the guys. He doesn't yet know where things are or how we operate at this department. We review scenarios that can happen during the shift and the kinds of calls we typically get at this hour—things like car fires, assisting fire departments in neighboring towns, or responding to false alarms. It's important for us always to be thinking and talking about our jobs.

Suddenly we get a call from the dispatcher. It's an announcement that there's a fire and the address of where we need to go. It's a structure fire, meaning it's an actual burning building. It's an apartment building on one of the main roads in town only about four blocks from the firehouse. We jump into the fire rig—a truck that pumps water and carries the firefighters and hoses—and go.

As soon as we pull onto the street and steer toward the building, we see the fire in the air. I see the header, which is a plume of black smoke and fire, rising sixty feet high. During the short, four-block drive, we hear the police dispatch over the radio about the fire. There are people trapped inside the burning building and the police are already on the scene.

As we pull up, I see the fire coming out of the second-floor window. The flames are reaching up past the third floor and onto the roof of the three-story building. I notice that there's a small office business on the ground floor and apartments on the second and third floors. Our first concern when we arrive at a fire is to search for living people. Then we want to save as

Lieutenant Jeff Kraft

much of the building and surrounding structures as possible. The first-floor office is closed and dark. Plus it's below the origin of the fire, so we don't have to worry about it too much since fire spreads upward. We know there are people

on the upper floors, so that's where I plan to go first.

I jump out of the truck and meet the police officer who arrived just before us. He says that some of the residents from the apartments escaped from the building and told him that there are people trapped on the third floor. My engineer gets to work on preparing the waterline and hooking up to a nearby hydrant, while the new firefighter calls for backup. I have all of my fire gear on at this point. I'm wearing boots, fire-resistant pants and coat, helmet, fire-resistant gloves, and my air pack. I put my air mask over my face and kick in the door that opens to the stairway leading up to the apartments. Our policy—and the policy of most fire departments—is never to go on a search alone in a burning building. At the very least, have another firefighter around with a hose to protect the stairwell, in case the fire spreads. But as I enter the burning building, I ask myself, *If that was my family up there, would I want someone to wait to save them?* I go in alone.

I climb up the stairs to the second floor and stop on the landing. There's an apartment to my right, another straight down the hall, and a third to my left. I know the apartment to the left is where the fire is. The door is wide open and the flames are roaring inside. I can see the heavy smoke pouring into the hallway.

. . . I ask myself, If that was my family up there, would I want someone to wait to save them? I go in alone.

The stairway to the third floor is between where I'm standing and that burning apartment. Black smoke is rushing right up the staircase to the top floor. I'm able to close the door of the burning apartment to prevent any more smoke from going up those stairs. It buys me some time. I'm looking all around and asking myself questions about the situation: How much has the fire burned? How much more time do I have before the fire causes the floors or walls to collapse? I note the layout of the building and try to figure out my options for rescue, escape, and containing the fire.

I climb up through the black smoke to the third floor. I can't see anything through the smoke, so I take each step slowly as I feel my way up the stairs. Every few steps, I stop and hold my breath. I want to concentrate on listening for voices without my breath making an echoing sound in the mask, which covers my whole face. I can hear a muffled sound, like a grunt or soft cry. At the top of the stairs, I reach down and feel that there's a woman lying on the floor.

I throw her arm around my neck. She's disoriented, confused, and having trouble breathing. I make a judgment call and take off my air mask to put it over the woman's face. A firefighter is never supposed to take off an air mask. If I breathe in too much smoke, I might become another person who needs to be rescued rather than the person doing the rescuing. But this woman is in bad shape and needs the air. I know that once I get her down the stairs, she'll be able to breathe again. She's a small, light woman, so it's not too difficult for me to pick her up. Holding her body in my arms, I move as quickly as I can down the stairs through the smoke. I make myself take short, little breaths. The mistake people often make in smoke is to take deep breaths. This makes things much worse.

Once we're on the second floor, we're below the rising smoke, so it's easier to breathe again. I take the woman down the last flight of stairs and outside to where the police officers can take care of her until the ambulance arrives.

I put my air mask back on and rush up the stairs. Back on the

third floor, I find an apartment with the door half open. Inside I see there's a closed bedroom door. I open the door and find a man inside standing by his open window. He has good air where he's standing, so he's doing okay. I explain to him that I have to get him out of the building. Again, I share my air to help get him through the thick, black smoke on the third floor. In addition to rescuing him, my job is to keep him calm. I let him know I'm here to help him and that I'm going to lead him out to safety. Panic is the real enemy in these situations. I put his arm around my neck and quickly guide him down the two flights of stairs and outside. I'm lucky—he's moving quickly and he's under control.

By now my engineer has the attack waterline ready. The hose is connected to the fire hydrant, with water ready to flow. So I grab the nozzle on the end of the hose, what we call "the pipe." By this time, other fire departments from surrounding communities have arrived. I send a few of those firefighters up to the third floor to make sure no one else is up there. I run back into the building, pulling the hose up to the second floor and to the apartment on the left, where the fire is contained. I open the door—my fire-resistant gloves allow me to do this. The whole place smells like a campfire as wood crackles, pops, and burns around me. I turn on the water at the nozzle, and with the hose I get the fire under control quickly. I spray up and down the walls and ceiling until the fire is mostly out and the burnt wood smokes from just having been on fire.

I go back downstairs as other firefighters head upstairs to finish the job. I'm tired at this point, and it's best to get a fresh set of eyes to look everything over. They'll make sure the fire is fully extinguished.

I'm back outside in the fresh air, and it takes a while for everything to sink in. Once the fire is fully out, we clean up and put away the hoses and gear. I'm able to think about exactly what has just happened. I saved two lives. It's a feeling that doesn't quite register at first. I remember the words of a firefighter who was my mentor. He once told me after a fire we fought together, "You know, you get one or two opportunities in your life to make a real impact. The decisions you make determine whether that person can tell the story of how they survived the fire. The reactions you make during those short moments, you can't ever redo, and you may get only one shot to make a difference in someone's life. When that chance comes, you have to take it."

After the fire, an investigation revealed that the cause was children playing with lighters and matches in the apartment that was burned out. For his bravery in fighting this fire, LIEUTENANT JEFF KRAFT was awarded the 2005 Fireslayer of the Year Award, a national honor given by the safety device manufacturer MSA. In 2006, the governor of Illinois gave Lieutenant Kraft the state's Medal of Honor for his acts of bravery on April 15, 2005.

WHAT IT'S LIKE ...
To Walk Across America

NAME: Joe Hurley
DATES: March–December 2004
LOCATION: Provincetown,
Massachusetts, to Long Beach,
California, along Route 6

Twenty miles a day, five days a week: That's the pace I need to keep in order to walk the 3,500-mile journey along Route 6, which runs almost entirely across the United States of America. That's the pace I need to keep so that I don't end up in the Colorado Rocky Mountains during the threat of snow, which can come as early as October. During the trip, I travel with a photographer who drives a car. He picks me up at the end of each day's walk, then drops me off at the same place the next day to walk another twenty miles. Many people all over the country have heard about my challenge. I'm fortunate to have some hotels, inns, and friends offer me free places to sleep, though sometimes I have to pay for lodging.

It's March 25, 2004. I'm in Provincetown, Massachusetts, at the very tip of Cape Cod. I am nervous and excited, just like I'd feel at the beginning of any big sporting event. There is so much I have to plan. I need to make sure that I've packed the right clothes and that I have everything I may need. It's going to be many months before I'm home again, so there's a lot to check before I get started. My wife and daughter are with me, and they will see me off tomorrow. It's hard to be focused on the walk at this point. I'm going to miss my family, and I want to spend the last few hours with them.

On March 26, I start walking toward Long Beach, California.

I grew up in Boston. I've been around Cape Cod before, but only in the summer, when it's a lively place. It's much different in the colder months. Very few people are around and some streets are completely empty.

When you're riding in a car at seventy miles per hour, the scenery flies by so quickly that you don't have time to take in the details. Walking, I see things I would have otherwise missed, like the emptiness of Cape Cod in the winter. The old houses and buildings are more than just flashes of color. I can see their details and character: their signs, decorations, plants, unique lawn ornaments— all the things you miss when you have less than a second to look.

Only ten miles in, I say to myself, *I can't do this. What was I thinking?* It hits me just how big this journey will be. Ten miles in and I'm already tired. How can I make it 3,500 miles? I think, *People are going to laugh if this guy who was going to walk across the country couldn't even walk off Cape Cod!* I decide that my first goal is to walk through all of Cape Cod. That would be better than nothing, right? Then if I have to give up, at least I would have accomplished something.

I have a pack with me that contains snacks and water to drink. When I'm hungry, I sometimes stop for food at restaurants or I just pick up a few things from grocery stores. Because I'm burning so many calories, I don't have to watch what I eat too much, but I want to eat good kinds of foods with proteins and carbohydrates so that I have the energy to keep walking.

It takes me three days to make my way off the Cape and into the rest of Massachusetts. The weather is cold. Even so, I'm sweating while I'm walking. I wear socks on my hands—this is an old runner's trick. They keep my hands warm and allow me to wipe the sweat from my brow.

With Cape Cod behind me, I try to think about getting to Rhode Island. If I can just make it out of Massachusetts, that will be something to talk about.

For the next four days I walk through southeastern Massachusetts. Some of the towns are small and I don't see anyone during the walk. Cities like New

Bedford are busy, and at times I need to stop for traffic lights. Finally I reach East Providence, Rhode Island. I've got one state down.

I have a lot of time to think during the walk. I think about my life, my family, and the work I've done, but mostly I think about walking. I'm also getting pretty good at judging distances. I count how many steps I take in a mile: 2,500. I figure that to cross the United States, it will take me about 10 million steps. But I can't think about that when I'm still in Rhode Island.

Once I step into Connecticut, I think about my next big goal: to make it to the New York state line. If I do that, I can say I made it out of New England. The Connecticut stretch of Route 6 is familiar to me. Several years ago I walked the road for a series of newspaper articles I was writing. During that walk I discovered that Route 6 runs almost entirely across the United States. I made that first walk to discover the small towns across the state that I had never heard of before.

Not everyone is pleasant during my travel. I'm in Newtown, Connecticut, and it's raining like crazy. It's a real storm. I'm wearing my rain gear and fighting the wind. Route 6 is a major roadway, but no one stops their car to ask if I need help. Not one police car drives by to see if I'm okay. I'm not actually expecting people to stop, but I'm surprised that no one even asks if I need help. Maybe I look too weird walking in this weather. I'm wearing a trash bag for a raincoat.

I step into New York on April 22, and I think, *Well, I walked all the way through New England. If I don't finish the whole walk, at least I can say I did that.* I decide I will look at my walk in stages. *If I can just get through New York,* and then, *If I can just get through Pennsylvania . . .* These goals are easier to think about achieving than the big one.

As I walk through Pennsylvania, I think, *I'll make sure I get to Cleveland. If I get there, well, then I'll be the guy who walked from the Atlantic Ocean to Cleveland. You can't really laugh at him too much! That will be an accomplishment.* In Pennsylvania I buy some new shoes. My first pair are worn out and falling apart.

In some places, people join me on my journey. As I walk into Meadville, Pennsylvania, five or ten people come along. Someone asks, "Are you that guy walking across the country? Can we come along?" The group slows me down a bit, but the company helps pass the time. They mostly ask about the trip so far and why I'm doing this. My standard answer is that I want to see if people across the country have changed from what I remember from my childhood. Are people today different from how they were when I was a boy? But a bigger reason is probably

because the challenge is there—the United States is there for me to walk across, and I want to see if I can do it. A few people walk with me for most of the day before they get picked up to go home, back to their lives.

It's late May, and the weather is heating up. I'm having trouble finding a good hat to protect me from the sun. Baseball caps keep the sun out of my eyes, but they don't cover the back of my neck, which is starting to burn. I try one of those hats that look kind of like a baseball cap with the drape in the back to cover your neck, but wind from passing trucks blows the hat off my head. I try a straw sombrero with a string around the neck. This also gets blown off my head. Finally I settle on a cloth and leather cowboy hat—this hat covers my face and the back of my neck, and doesn't blow off my head easily. I must look weird. How many people do you see walking down the street in a cowboy hat and shorts? But I can't worry about that. I need to wear the gear that suits me best for my walk.

So far, I've managed to avoid blisters, sprains, and other injuries. One night in Pennsylvania, though, the trip almost ends for me.

I'm taking a bath in the hotel room and I leave my belt on the floor beside the tub. The bath helps relax my aching muscles, and I soon forget about where I am and what I'm doing. When I get out of the tub, I step onto the prong of my belt buckle, which is facing up. The metal piece sinks right into my skin. The pain is horrible, and I'm bleeding. I say to myself, *The walk is over right here.* But I bandage up my foot and take a walk around the room.

. . . because the challenge is there—the United States is there for me to walk across, and I want to see if I can do it.

Each step fires pain all the way up my leg. I'm so disappointed when I go to bed that night. I can't believe this could be the end of the trip. The next morning my foot still hurts, but not as badly as the night before. I decide I'm not stopping. I start to walk. There's some blood in my sock, and my foot still hurts, but I keep walking. Each day the pain is less, and I know I can keep on going.

I finally make it to Cleveland and tell myself, *If I make it to Chicago, then I will have made it to the Midwest—almost halfway!*

In Indiana there are long stretches of flat, empty roads. But soon there are towns, then bigger towns, more people and cars, and soon I'm on the south side of Chicago. Provincetown to Chicago *is* something to talk about. But there's still a long way to go, and I'm only on my third pair of shoes.

As the summer wears on, I think about Colorado. My whole strategy for this walk is based around getting to the Rocky Mountains before fall. There's a section of road in Colorado called Loveland Pass that sits about twelve thousand feet above sea level. It's the highest pass in the Colorado Rockies, and mostly uphill. If I don't cross that by the end of September, the road may be covered with snow and I may not make it.

I arrive at Loveland Pass on September 6. Walking this stretch of road is similar to how I pictured it would be, except it's more dangerous. There are spots where there is no place to walk, and tractor-trailers whiz by. Also, in higher elevations, the air is thinner. Breathing is more difficult up here, but I adjust after a while. It's a full day's walk up to the top and back down the other side. The walk up *is* exhausting, but I expect it to be difficult, so I am ready.

The walk back down is actually more difficult because of all the impact on my knees and tired legs. When I reach the bottom I feel so tired, but also renewed. With the highest part of the Colorado Rockies behind me, I feel like I can make it the rest of the way. The worst is behind me.

In Utah, people warn me about a hill called Soldier Summit. It's called that because in July 1861, a group of Confederate soldiers got caught at the top of the mountain in a snowstorm. A few of them died and are still buried there. People tell me it's going to be tough. I think, *How tough could it be? I've been across the Rockies!*

It's mid-October when I reach the town at the bottom of Soldier Summit: Helper, Utah. The town was named that because it was where an extra railroad engine used to be placed on trains to help them get over the hill. That should have given me some idea of the challenge ahead of me.

Like most mountain roads, this one has tight, steep curves. I get up the first one and say to myself, "Gee, this isn't so bad." Of course, the road turns another curve and goes back up again . . . and again . . . and again. I spend the whole day thinking the top of the hill is going to be right around the next corner. I walk ten to fifteen miles uphill. It's a long and exhausting day. The next day I make the journey down the other side. It's not as physically tiring, but it's mentally challenging. I need to pay attention to where I step so that I don't slip, blow out an ankle, or hurt my knees with the impact. Soldier Summit turns out to be the worst hill of the entire trip.

I think, How tough could it be? I've been across the Rockies!

With so much of the country behind me now, I can focus on finishing my trip. There are just two states in front of me: Nevada and California. It's November, and I think I'm still on track to make it to the Pacific Ocean in December.

I wear out my sixth pair of shoes in Nevada.

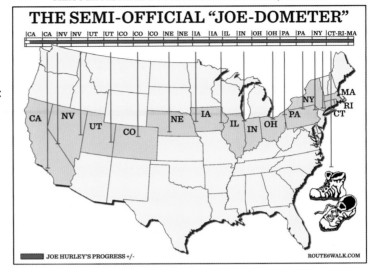

U.S. ROUTE 6 TRAVELS COAST-TO-COAST
THROUGH 14 STATES & OVER 500 COMMUNITIES...3,600 MILES

THE SEMI-OFFICIAL "JOE-DOMETER"

JOE HURLEY'S PROGRESS +/-   ROUTE6WALK.COM

I've lost about twenty-five pounds on this trip, and my clothes need to be safety-pinned together in places. My legs just hurt all of the time. It's a dull pain, the kind you feel after participating in a big sporting event. This pain doesn't go away, though, because I don't have time to really rest my legs.

Crossing into California, I start to think about the finish, about being done with this walk. I'm not looking at the scenery as much as I did months ago when I began. I just want to finish and go home.

I'm about ten miles from Long Beach, California, and the Pacific Ocean, and I realize this is going to be the last day of my walk: December 9, 2004. As close as I am, I feel like I may not actually finish. It sounds silly, but I have such an urge to stop that I feel like I might. Every part of me is aching. My toes hurt, my back hurts, everything hurts. But I know I've come too far. I can smell the ocean. I know how disappointed I would be if I stopped so close to the end. I just think

Joe Hurley touching the Pacific Ocean

about putting one foot in front of the other and walking. Step, step, step. It's only when I get to the last five miles of my journey that I'm sure I will make it.

I have half a mile to go when my wife, Pat, meets me to walk the rest of the way by my side. I'm so glad to see her again—she gives me a long hug that feels so good. Though she's come out to meet me a few times during my long walk, I know this time we get to stay together. I'm excited and thrilled—it's almost over! There's a bunch of people at the pier where I'm supposed to finish. My family and some friends are there, along with some members of the press and a few spectators. They have champagne and they're cheering for me.

I see the ocean! I'm a little distracted by the people and excitement, and by knowing it's almost over. But I'm determined to finish this right. I walk past the end of the road and onto the pier. I reach the end and dip my hand in the Pacific. The feeling isn't what I expected. I'm just glad to be done. I've made it.

I see the ocean!

[On his journey, JOE HURLEY walked through Massachusetts, Rhode Island, Connecticut, New York, Pennsylvania, Ohio, Indiana, Illinois, Iowa, Nebraska, Colorado, Utah, Nevada, and California. Joe calculates that he took 10 million steps across the United States of America. He is writing a book about his cross-country walk.]

WHAT IT'S LIKE . . .
To Survive a Tornado

NAME: Linda Robbins
DATE: May 12, 2004
LOCATION: Attica, Kansas

Our house is still under construction. The cabinets, plumbing, and electricity are in, but we still have the flooring and some other work to finish inside. My husband, Randy, and I are doing the entire inside work ourselves. We're about six weeks away from moving in. We currently live across town and are looking forward to making this new place home.

It's a beautiful day in May—the sun is shining and it's just a gorgeous late afternoon. I'm working on finishing the bathroom door, and I decide to take a break and walk out on the back deck. I look out and see a group of people standing on the overpass on Route 160, which is close to our house. They're all looking in the same direction at something. I think, *This is odd.* But it's a beautiful, calm day, so I don't give it another thought.

Suddenly Randy comes rushing up behind me. He says, "Aren't you afraid of tornadoes?" I just look at him, confused. He takes me around to the front of the house and I see this dark wall of black clouds. They are gathering straight across the sky, and there's a large section of clouds that are lower than the rest. Then I see the tornado form. I see the dirt in the field start to swirl about a half mile away from where I'm standing. I've seen dirt devils in the distance before, but something is different about this one. Then a funnel starts to form from the low-standing clouds and joins together with the swirl of dirt. The funnel grows bigger and bigger. Randy shouts, "We better get inside!" as hail starts to fall.

This is the average size of the hailstones that fell during the May 2004 Attica, Kansas, tornado.

From inside our house we watch through our front windows. The funnel keeps growing larger and larger. It's massive. My heart speeds up, but having grown up in the area, I know a tornado can form quickly and just disappear or go in another direction. But then I realize that the reason it looks like it's growing larger is because it's getting closer—it's maybe a quarter mile away now. Randy yells, "It's going to hit us. We better get to the basement!"

I know we should take cover immediately, but I am concerned that I left the window open in our first-floor bathroom. I don't want rain or debris to fly in, so I run through the foyer and down a short hallway to the bathroom. I try to open the door, but the wind is so strong coming through the open bathroom window that it's pushing back against the door. I can't force it open. Suddenly the front door of the house blows open from the tornado's wind. Randy gets his body in between the door and the wall and puts his

"It's going to hit us. We better get to the basement!"

two feet on the wall. He uses the force of his entire body to try to close the front door. He hollers at me, "Come on! Come on!" I run toward him, confused, and he yells again, "Let's get to the basement!"

Randy and I run down the hall and fling open the basement door. We rush in, shut the door, and get down into the corner of the basement behind the stairs. Randy and I just hold each other and catch our breaths. I'm nervous, but I think we're safe. I don't quite know how to feel because I've never experienced a tornado before. Randy has. He's holding me close and won't let go.

Our house is made of Styrofoam and cement. The Styrofoam pads the outside of the cement structure. The thick walls are quiet and strong—I believe they will protect us. I hear wind rushing around us, but it's not that loud. We have glass

doors in the basement that lead to the outside, and suddenly I hear them blow in, shattering. I can't see them break because we're hiding under the stairs and my view of everything is blocked. Now I'm afraid. I realize our house might be breaking around us.

In a matter of seconds, it's all over. It's really quiet now.

The roof blowing off of the Robbins' house

I start to pull away from Randy to go back upstairs. He won't let me go and says, "If that was the eye of the storm, there is going to be more. . . . just wait a minute." We wait in the basement for a few more minutes, but it's still quiet. Then we hear people yelling and talking outside. From their conversation I can tell it's a team of storm chasers. Because there were two trucks parked outside, the storm chasers believed there may have been people inside the house when it was hit. They circle around our house as they yell for us. We hear them only when they reach the broken glass door and see us inside and crouching under the stairs. They come in and ask if we are okay. They stay with us in the basement for a little while to make sure the storm is really over. They're very concerned for us and relieved to learn that we were the only people in the house at the time the tornado hit. They say they saw and filmed what happened to our house during the storm.

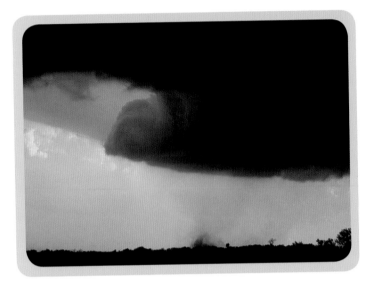

By the time we go back outside, it's dark. The sun is now setting and the thick clouds from the storm are still over us. It's difficult to see the full extent of the damage. From our front lawn we can see that the old shop building on the property that once belonged to Randy's grandfather is completely gone. Papers, splinters of wood, and other debris are scattered like confetti all around us. The old shop building contained a lot of items from Randy's childhood. He had old photographs of his family, toys, paperwork, some of his grandfather's tools, and all kinds of other items. So many memories are now scattered everywhere.

The roof has been torn off our house and is lying in the field where the tornado came from. It is still mostly in one piece; it was plucked off the house and dropped on the ground, so it looks like a house has been buried. Our house looks so strange with four walls but no roof. Every window in our house is busted, and the front deck, where I was standing when I discovered the storm, is gone.

The entire face of the front wall of our house was bricked. That brick wall is now on the ground, in one solid piece, and upside-down. So it was torn from the side of our house and completely flipped over.

Before the storm, I had parked my pickup truck facing north on the driveway. Now it's facing south. Randy's pickup truck now has a two-by-four piece of wood sticking through its door like a spear.

Debris and housing insulation were thrown everywhere. A three-pronged garden tool sticks out from a door that's leaning against a wall. Everything is in shambles around us.

We watch the video that the storm chasers filmed of the tornado hitting our house on the playback on their video cameras. They were positioned about a half mile down the road from our house and caught everything on tape. The tornado destroyed only our house and ripped up some of the surrounding fields. The twister was headed toward some neighborhoods down the road, but the storm chasers believe the large overpass near our house helped break up the storm before it did any more damage.

Thirty-seven seconds was all it took to do all this damage. I realize then that I wasn't scared during the storm because it all happened so fast. But when I see the part of the video where our roof comes off the house, it hits me: we could have died in there. I thank God we weren't living in the house yet. None of our everyday stuff is here, and neither of us is hurt. We work so hard to build our homes and fill it with stuff, and I realize it can all be taken away in just thirty-seven seconds. But stuff can be replaced—Randy and I cannot.

LINDA AND RANDY ROBBINS rebuilt their home in Attica, Kansas, and are still living there today, though they always keep their eyes on the sky to look for a dangerous storm that could turn into another angry tornado.

WHAT IT'S LIKE . . .

To Fly with the
U.S. Air Force Thunderbirds

NAME: Major Tyrone Douglas
DATE: March 15, 2008
LOCATION: San Angelo, Texas

Early in the season, I always get a little nervous walking out to the jet. It's like getting ready for a big football or basketball game or the first day of school. I am a Thunderbird pilot, and today is the first day of our new season. I'm thinking about the routine and how to run everything well so that the show looks good for the crowd. I focus on that as I climb into the cockpit.

Once I'm in the jet, I feel like I'm in familiar territory because I've been a pilot for years. My nerves start to settle down. I start up the jet's engines and smell those familiar exhaust smells; it's a little like burning oil. The engine makes the entire jet vibrate, like it's alive and ready to roar. It's exciting, and I

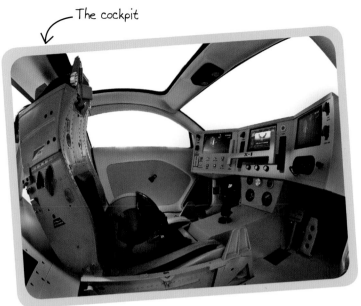

The cockpit

can feel the machine—it's almost like I'm a part of it. Plus, I know what this thing can do once I'm in the air. There's raw power at my fingertips.

I give the engine a little bit of thrust to taxi, rolling the plane out past the crowd toward the runway. I can see people cheering and waving in the stands. Though I have practiced this routine many times, it's the first time many of these folks are seeing it. This gets me excited. I wave back, pump my fist in the air, get comfortable in the cockpit, and taxi toward the runway a short distance away from the crowd. There are six planes in total in our air show.

First up, four F-16 Thunderbirds take off together ahead of me in a diamond formation—one plane in the front,

About to take off

Diamond formation

two side-by-side behind the leader, and one behind and in between the pair, bringing up the rear. Once they clear the runway and are in the air, I take off.

Communication between the Thunderbirds is critical. We're on our radios to one another constantly throughout the program. The four jets that stay in mainly a diamond formation fly within three feet of each other for most of the forty-five-minute program. The boss, or lead jet in the formation, has to let the other three pilots know exactly what he's doing—when he's making a left turn, when he's making a right turn, and how much he's pulling back on the stick. They have to follow him precisely.

I'm one of two solo pilots—that is, pilots who get to fly independent of the formation. I get this big adrenaline rush as the engine roars and I go from zero

to two hundred miles per hour in about fifteen seconds. Right off the runway, I show the maximum performance of the F-16. That's why the Thunderbirds are at this air show—to show the American people, and the world, how fast, agile, and powerful our jets are.

I take the plane immediately into a steep climb straight up that pushes my body through about nine Gs, or nine times the force of gravity. I weigh about 200 pounds, so when I'm under nine times the force of gravity in the jet, it's like I weigh about 1,800 pounds. The force puts a lot of strain on my muscles, especially my neck. I have to be in good shape to fly with the Thunderbirds. I exercise regularly and eat right. "Pulling Gs" constantly for forty-five minutes takes a toll on my body.

I take the plane immediately into a steep climb straight up that pushes my body through about nine Gs, or nine times the force of gravity.

Our planes go incredibly fast. My top speed during the air show is Mach .94, or about 620 miles per hour. Mach 1 is the speed of sound, and we stay just under the sound barrier to be safe. If we hit Mach 1, the sonic boom would bust eardrums on the ground and break any windows within a few miles.

After my vertical climb, I roll the jet wing-over-wing, and fly back across the runway just a few hundred feet off the ground, right over the crowd.

Once all six planes are in the air and have done some basic flying tricks, the other solo pilot and I approach each other in the air, head-on. We have to fly toward each other at five hundred miles per hour, which is a "closing speed" of one thousand miles per hour. We must have good communication and perfect timing, or else. The approach happens quickly, and for the crowd it looks like we're going to fly into each other and collide. We get real close, then suddenly break in opposite directions and race past each other. Success!

The maneuver I think is most exciting is coming up. This is when the other solo pilot and I fly over the crowd starting from an altitude of seven thousand feet. We fly about five hundred feet apart side by side and come barreling down like a roller coaster from behind the crowd. Once we hit five hundred feet above the crowd's heads, we bottom out, fly past the crowd side by side, and then turn

toward each other and cross paths. From the crowd's perspective it looks like we're going to collide. We pass each other within eighty feet. On the ground, the crowd lets out a giant gasp, and then a sigh of relief. I've seen this trick performed when I used to sit in the audience. It looks amazing from the ground.

Though this is one of the least complicated parts of the show, it looks very impressive from the ground when all six planes pull into a tight formation. We perform this near the end of our program. With smoke trailing behind us, we pull the jets into a giant roll. Just a few feet separate each plane as we make the loop.

For the entire show, I need to stay 100 percent focused on what I'm doing. The routine isn't just taxing physically, but mentally as well. The timing, the communication—everything has to go right. When you're flying at 550 miles per hour, there's no room for error. This job requires great communication and a lot of trust among the people you're flying with. The jet is incredibly expensive, and there are thousands of people watching on the ground. Throughout the performance I stay focused on getting the routine right, giving a good show, and keeping myself, my team, and the folks on the ground safe at all times.

I'm back on the ground now, and I can see the crowd's reaction as I step out of the cockpit. This is one of the most rewarding parts of the job and the reason

I joined the team. I walk through the autograph line and I see an eight-year-old boy who tells me this was the best show he has ever seen. Some of the kids just see me and say, "Wow," their mouths wide-open in awe. There are grandparents for whom this is the first air show they've attended and had no idea what our jets were capable of. I see other folks who beam with pride because we represent *their* country, *their* military. I realize I am a positive role model for them—someone they can look up to.

Major Tyrone Douglas signing an
autograph for a fan

The Thunderbirds have been the official demonstration team of the United States Air Force
since 1953. They exhibit the capabilities of USAF airplanes and pilots by doing air shows all
across the country. The Thunderbirds are an elite group, and each pilot is on the team for only
two years. MAJOR TYRONE DOUGLAS is the first African American to be a lead solo pilot
in the Thunderbirds.

WHAT IT'S LIKE...
To Blast Off into Space

Name: Sandra H. Magnus, Ph.D.
Dates: October 7–18, 2002
Location: Space Shuttle
Atlantis, Kennedy Space Center,
Florida

We go out to the launch pad a couple of hours before the flight's departure time. The crew and I stand at the bottom of the elevator and look up at this huge vehicle that we're going to ride into space. This is something I've wanted to do my whole life, and here I am—about to fly into space for the first time. I'm excited, but also concerned with doing my job correctly. I am a NASA astronaut.

The elevator takes us up 195 feet to the entranceway to the space shuttle. The seven crew members go in one by one. I'm the last one to board because I'm Mission Specialist 2; my seat is slightly behind and between the pilot's and commander's seats. I have a chance to look at the space shuttle while I'm waiting.

The shuttle looks big from here. It's strong, powerful, and protected with a thick, white layer of heat-resistant ceramic tiles. There are all kinds of noises around me. The gases that fill the shuttle's large tanks are really cold, so there's always some water vapor floating around us on the launch pad. I hear a lot of hissing, and it seems almost like the vehicle is alive and eager to go.

Finally I climb into the orbiter, which—as its name implies—is what detaches from the launcher and circles in the orbit around the earth. This is where the entire crew will live and work for almost eleven days. The area where we sit is compact. There's just enough room for seven seats. There are computers and switches all around us that tell us what the orbiter is doing and if systems are okay. They also allow us to communicate with people on the ground at NASA.

The NASA staff helps us put our parachutes on and then straps us into our seats. When the space shuttle is ready for launch, it looks like an airplane pointing straight up. So when we sit in our seats, we lie on our backs and look to the front of the orbiter and at the

The crew entering Space Shuttle *Atlantis*

sky above. Everyone in the flight crew puts helmets on after we're strapped into our seats, and now we're all ready to go. I can't see it, but I hear the door close. It means we're one step closer to blastoff.

There's still about an hour and a half to go until launch and I'm just waiting in the orbiter. It seems like time slows down. I'm anticipating the big moment while we check all of the systems and do our jobs.

Finally we get to the last ten minutes before the launch, and

Dr. Sandra Magnus is ready for blast-off.

time seems to speed up again. Those ten minutes seem more like two. Everything happens very quickly with our preparations for liftoff. We check and recheck our computers and systems. We make sure we're secure in our seats and that our clipboards, books, and everything else is properly stowed. At T-minus two minutes, I close the visor on my helmet and I think, *Oh my gosh, here we go!*

At this point it's like my mind splits in two. Part of my brain is paying attention to the computers, making sure that the systems look okay and that we've covered everything. The other part of my brain is bouncing with excitement, thinking, *We're going to space, we're going to space, we're going to space!*

I'm not afraid, just fired up. A month or two ago, I went through all those thoughts of what can go wrong. Of course I remember the past space shuttle accidents that happened in recent history. But at T-minus two minutes, I'm just thrilled, yet focused on my tasks.

There's also this growing anticipation because I don't know exactly what's going to happen. I mean, I've done practice takeoffs many times before, so I sort of know. But this time it's for real. This time I'm going into orbit.

Six seconds before launch and the main engines on the shuttle are lit to make sure they're functioning correctly. If something is wrong at this point, Flight Control can still cancel the flight.

The engines are at the very aft, or rear, of the shuttle, so I really don't hear them. They sound only like a dull roar to me. The whole stack—the shuttle and solid rocket boosters—starts to sway from the force, but we're still bolted down to the launch platform. They haven't yet blown the pyrotechnics, which are controlled explosions that release the solid rocket boosters, so we're just swaying to the dull roar. Before I even realize it, six seconds go by and T-equals zero. The solid rocket boosters light.

The solid rocket boosters, or SRBs, provide 6 million of the 7 million pounds of force that the shuttle needs to be thrust into space. Once the SRBs ignite, we're definitely going somewhere because you can't turn them off.

But this time it's for real.
This time I'm going into orbit.

The noise inside the orbiter increases twenty times. The rockets are so powerful that they make so much noise and vibrate everything.

Then the pyrotechnics on the launch pad blow and it feels like somebody has just kicked the chair I'm sitting in. I feel a huge jolt even though I know the shuttle just gracefully moves away from the ground. It's not like we leap off the launch pad, but the pyrotechnics feels like a kick to get us going. Then I feel pressure on my chest—about one and a half times G, or the normal amount of gravity.

The noise is roaring now. It sounds like being in the middle of a huge tunnel of cars. Everything is vibrating pretty violently. I can still read the computer screens, but the seats and equipment are shaking. This is the most dramatic part of our climb into space, but all I can do is rattle in my seat and keep checking our systems to make sure everything is functioning properly.

Just two minutes into the flight, all of the fuel in the SRBs is used up. We're thirty miles up and ready for the orbiter to separate from the SRBs. Suddenly I see a flash out the front windows, and I hear a loud bang. I'm startled—we didn't simulate the noise of the explosion, so I'm surprised. But when the SRBs detach from our orbiter, all of the violent vibration stops. The sound goes back to the dull roar I heard at T-minus six seconds. It's two minutes into the flight and we've already got the boost we need to get us off the planet.

I have a mirror on my wrist that I can use to look behind me as we are climbing into space. I can see the earth dropping away below us. At first, the earth looks just like it does from an airplane. You can see the same kinds of things: the objects on the ground get smaller and smaller; highways turn into thin lines and then disappear; I can see more and more of the coastline of Florida. But as we get higher and higher, I can start to see the curve of the earth, the horizon, and the atmosphere. One thing that amazes me is how thin our atmosphere is. We have such a thin shell of air around our planet that supports us. Everyone, including myself, takes it for granted. To see it is incredible. It makes the planet look so delicate and fragile, and it's very beautiful.

We're flying on the shuttle's three main engines now and will continue to do so for the next six minutes. The flight is much smoother now. I continue to check the computers and occasionally look out the window as we climb.

Just as we're nearing our orbit, I start to feel like I'm about three times my weight—three Gs. It's because the shuttle is accelerating to push us into orbit. Experiencing three Gs is like having a gorilla sit on your chest. You have to force air out of your lungs in order to talk. Breathing is difficult because you really have to work to fill your lungs with enough air. Thankfully, this lasts for only thirty seconds.

Then, eight and a half minutes after leaving the ground, we've finally reached our orbit. We're traveling at more than seventeen thousand miles per hour, and we're about one hundred miles up. Now our orbiter acts like a satellite—the earth's gravity holds us from drifting off into space, and we begin circling the planet. During liftoff, the shuttle climbed in a big arc, so when we reach orbit, the top of the shuttle is facing earth, and the bottom is facing out toward space. Though we're upside down, I can't feel it because we're in zero gravity.

All of a sudden the engines cut off, it's very quiet, and I realize I'm not sitting in my seat anymore. Well, I'm attached to my seat by a harness, but there's no contact between the seat and my body. *This is so strange*, I think. An astronaut carries a procedure book at all times. It has checklists of gauges, computer readings, and warning lights we're supposed to watch as we go into orbit. I simply let go of my book and it floats in front of me. I start giggling because it's just so neat.

We're settling into orbit, and it's a very busy time. We have to change the shuttle from a rocket

Having fun in zero gravity

into living quarters. We stow the seats, open the storage areas, and take out the gear that was secured before launch. I'm weightless at zero G, and everything becomes a little more difficult. For example, on earth, if

you set a pencil down on a table, it stays down—but not in space. It floats. There is no up or down in space. I have to put so much thought into doing simple tasks because things won't stay put.

I need to get out of my seat now, and I realize that if I'm completely detached from my harnesses, I will probably lose control of my body and bounce everywhere. I keep one of my harnesses attached and anchored to my seat. Zero gravity takes a lot of getting used to. I have to work to keep control of my body as I start to move around. I manage to remove my helmet and gloves and get them stowed away. I take some pens and pencils, get my procedure book ready, and push off to the back of the flight deck to open the big payload doors that run the entire length across the top of the shuttle.

As the doors open, I can see earth. I'm speechless. Our planet is so beautiful. It's blue and green, like in pictures, but it looks so peaceful, quiet, and inviting from up here. From space, earth looks like an oasis.

I see the islands in the Pacific Ocean along the volcano ring. The ocean is a host of colors. As I look closer to the areas where the islands are, the ocean's

depth starts changing and the color goes from deep, velvety midnight blue to navy blue to royal blue to sky blue to aquamarine blue to blue-green to green-blue. I see a whole rainbow of blues and greens.

 I feel so lucky to be up here. An astronaut's job is difficult but extraordinary. Very few people get to see earth this way. Even if I never get the chance to go into space again, just to have seen this view is amazing. During all my years of training, and even since I was a kid, I've always dreamed of this moment. And now here I am.

I see a whole rainbow of blues and greens.

The crew of the space shuttle *Atlantis*

SANDRA H. MAGNUS, Ph.D., has worked for NASA since 1996. The mission described in her story, STS-112 aboard the space shuttle *Atlantis*, lasted ten days, nineteen hours, and fifty-eight minutes. On her second mission, launched in November 2008, Dr. Magnus spent four and a half months aboard the International Space Station, then returned in March 2009.

WHAT IT'S LIKE . . .
To Be Struck by Lightning

Name: Phil Broscovak
Date: August 2005
Location: Vedauwoo, Wyoming

Edward's Crack on Walt's Wall in Vedauwoo, Wyoming, is a relatively simple climb. It's the perfect place to bring my wife, my kids, my nephew, and his girlfriend. With the exception of my wife, they're all beginners to rock climbing. First, I climb up the rock face two hundred feet—about two-thirds of the way to the top—using my own ropes and equipment. I pound anchors into the crag, or rock, near the top so that I can attach my rope for the others to make their climb up Edward's Crack. At the highest part of the climb, I'm about sixty feet from the top. Though I can see some clouds way off in the distance, it's a beautiful day for climbing.

I have two two-hundred-foot ropes tied together forming a large loop, which I've threaded through the anchor I've put in the granite wall. One climber attaches himself to one end of the rope while someone else holds the other end, taking in the slack as they climb. If the climber slips, he won't fall more than a foot or so because the person on the ground has the other end of the rope. From the ground, I coach each member of my family up and then back down the route I've just set up with the anchors and ropes. I tell them where to step, how to hold the ropes, how to get themselves up the rock, and how to get back down. When the second-to-last person in our group starts up, I can hear a clap of thunder in the distance, but I'm not too worried. By the

Edward's crack on Walt's Wall
in Vedauwoo, Wyoming

time the last person is near the top, though, I am very concerned—there is thunder all around us now. The storm looks much closer and it's moving fast, but I've climbed in bad weather before. My first priority is to get the last person in my family down the ropes to safety.

Once the last person is on the ground, I quickly climb up to collect my anchors and ropes off the climbing route. I figure it will take me only a few minutes to scale the wall, pull out my gear, and get back down. If I wait for the storm to pass, it could be hours of sitting here, and I don't want to leave my expensive equipment.

I reach my gear as the rain really starts to pick up. There's no delay between the flashes of lightning and the claps of thunder. This means the thunderstorm is right over my head. Now I'm scared. There are two ways for me to get out of this situation. I could climb sixty feet up to the top of the crag and walk back down the gentle slope of the side. But sixty feet up would take me closer to the storm and leave me more exposed. My other option lies sixty feet to my right, along a ledge in the face of the rock, where there is a fixed, bolted station for climbers set up by the park service. These are metal loops bolted into the rock that are there for climbers to attach their ropes. I make my way to that station dragging my two two-hundred-foot ropes behind me. When I reach the bolts, I thread the end of the ropes through the looped bolt hangers so I can rappel, or move safely down my rope to the ground. It's a quick way to the bottom.

This means the thunderstorm is right over my head. Now I'm scared.

In my hurry, I don't have time to coil up my climbing ropes on the ledge, so I tie the end of rope that I've dragged over to the metal bolt and start pulling the rest of the ropes from behind me. I run back over the slippery slope to the anchor station. It's raining pretty hard now. I'm covered in sweat and water, and I'm afraid.

With my ropes secure, I throw them over the side of the rock toward the ground. Instead, they land about twenty feet below in a little ledge jutting out from the side of the cliff that's quickly filling with rainwater. In my head I'm saying, *Oh God, Ben Franklin, Ben Franklin!* Thinking about his famous kite in a lightning storm, I realize the rope I was holding could conduct electricity, especially when dangling in water on one end and attached to metal on the other. I'll need to go free the ropes stuck on the ledge so that they hang freely to the bottom of the crag. Otherwise I can't rappel down all the way to safe ground and I'll be taking a big risk.

I rappel down to the little ledge and see there is another set of permanent bolts here. There's not much room on this ledge. I'm a traditional climber and a person who considers safety incredibly important. So I clip into the bolt with my own personal tether—a safety harness I use for security so that if I slip while fixing the ropes, I'll only fall a couple of feet.

I duck down to free my rope and see this bright flash of light about two feet away. I know exactly what the flash is. I actually see the lightning hit the rock right next to the bolts, and then this bizarre, bluish, Jell-O-like stuff spreads out from where the lightning struck and surrounds me. I hear a thunderous explosion that is louder than anything I've ever heard in my life. Electricity travels throughout my body and causes every muscle in my body to twitch at once. I feel like ten thousand wasps are stinging me from the inside. The pain is horrible, my body is in a complete spasm, and the energy from the strike throws me off the crag. Everything goes black . . .

. . . I faintly hear my wife and children screaming. They must think I'm dead. I'm completely limp and hanging by my tether off the face of the rock. I can see that my rope is now hanging all the way to the ground. I'm able to move again—my body parts seem to be working, so I grab for the rope and reattach my gear to it. My only concern is to get down and out of this storm. I quickly rappel the rest of the way to the ground.

My wife is trembling. "Are you okay?" she asks me. At the base, I find out that the lightning strike was so powerful that it also knocked my nephew and

his girlfriend to the ground because they were leaning against the rock. The storm is still dangerous, and I know we shouldn't stand here any longer. "Get to the car!" I yell to everyone.

We wait in the car for the storm to pass and then go back to collect the climbing gear. I'm dazed and a little stunned, but I tell myself and my family I'm okay.

The next morning comes and I can't stand up straight. I don't go to a doctor because I assume that since I'm alive, just dazed and confused, that I'm okay. Plus, I don't have any major burns or anything, so I don't think it's necessary to go see a doctor. Every muscle hurts like I'd been hit by a train. My mind is foggy, and I'm confused. I have lost hearing in one ear. I have a burn in my eyes from the bright flash, so I still see the lightning strike everywhere I look.

It's a week later. Sometimes I can't find the right words to say. When I'm writing I might forget how to spell simple words like *the* and *and*. My memory is off—I can't remember conversations I had ten minutes earlier. My body's internal thermostat is wacky. It might be hot outside, but I want to bundle up in a winter coat, or it could be a chilly evening and I'm perfectly comfortable in a T-shirt. I've done some research into what a lightning strike can do to a person. The reason I'm forgetful and a little off-kilter is because the powerful burst of electricity melted off the myelin sheaths, or fatty tissue surrounding my nerve endings, which act like insulation around an electric wire. If a human being's nerves are exposed, that person can basically short-circuit. These nerve pathways form when you do any activity over and over again. For example, when you learn to ride a bicycle, the nerves in your brain form pathways so that the activity eventually becomes part of your normal life. My body's nervous system will need to rewire itself if I'm going to make a full recovery.

It's three years later and I am doing much better. My hearing is okay, and I don't see the lightning flash everywhere I look. The biggest obstacle I faced was dramatic mood swings, especially around my family. There were times when I just wasn't me. My family was very understanding, but my recovery was difficult for them as well. Three years after the accident, my life has returned to normal, with one exception: I still go climbing and adventuring with my family, but I never take a storm for granted.

PHIL BROSCOVAK has fully recovered from his 2005 lightning strike. He currently lives in Colorado with his family and is still an avid rock climber.

WHAT IT'S LIKE . . .
To Walk to the North Pole

NAME: Angus Cockney
DATES: March 20–May 14, 1989
LOCATION: Eureka, Ellesmere
Island, Canada, to the
North Pole (600 miles)

I'm Inuit [in-oo-it], one of the Native people of North America. My people have lived in the cold northern climates for thousands of years. Being from the north, I have a lot of knowledge about the ice and snow. Surviving and thriving in extreme cold is what my people have done for thousands of years. Plus I'm a Canadian ski champion, so it's natural for me to join this Icewalk expedition to the North Pole since we will be cross-country skiing for most of the journey. I was asked to join Icewalk because I'm an expert skier and I know the terrain.

Besides the leader of the group, Robert Swan, and myself, there are six others on the team: Dr. Misha Malakhov from Russia, Graeme Joy of Australia, Arved Fuchs of Germany, Rupert Summerson from the United Kingdom, Hiroshi Onishi from Japan, and Daryl E. Roberts of the United States. We are all heading to the North Pole together.

It's March 20 when we embark from base camp on Ellesmere Island. The timing of this journey is important. During the spring, the sun doesn't ever set in this part of the world, so we'll have plenty of light for traveling. But if we leave too late in the season, the ice will be partially melted, making the journey too dangerous.

Angus Cockney skiing to the North Pole

The landscape from here to the North Pole is all ice and snow, open water, and pressure ridges in the ice. A pressure ridge is where giant floating sheets of ice collide together and form a steep hill. At the beginning of the expedition, I'm a bit nervous and insecure. I have a wife at home who is pregnant with our first child. Also, I've never done an expedition like this before. This is a challenging environment; it's bitterly cold, which can be dangerous.

I take those first steps heading north, and it's a defining moment. I'm confident, ready to meet this challenge. As I head off Ellesmere Island down a hill, I think, *This is it. We're taking our first steps. There's no turning back now or there won't be much of a story.*

The temperature is –61.6 degrees Fahrenheit (–52 degrees Celsius). To give an example of how cold this is, if you boiled a pot of water and threw the boiling water into the air, it would freeze before it hit the ground. We're lucky because the winds are calm. But it's still very cold. I'm prepared for this. I'm in good shape and I have the best coats and snow gear available to keep me warm. I know I can handle it. I'm wearing a backpack full of supplies: clothing, food, cooking tools, and other necessities. It weighs about 60 pounds. Plus, I'm towing a sled full of more supplies, like extra skis, my camera, and film—that's another 60 pounds. So in addition to the heavy gear I have to wear to keep me warm, I'm carrying 120 pounds of extra weight.

Each of us has enough food for ten days. We eat

. . . I think, *This is it. We're taking our first steps. There's no turning back now or there won't be much of a story.*

high-fat foods to give us plenty of calories to burn on our long journey. These are foods like porridge, butter, and whale blubber, which tastes really salty and has a consistency like beef jerky. If we run out of supplies, we have a radio that we can use to call back to base camp. An airplane is scheduled to fly over us every ten days and drop a parachute carrying more food, fuel, and blankets for us. But for those ten days in between, we're on our own to survive.

Our team cross-country skis north for eighteen hours per day. Skiing that far each day takes a great deal of energy and concentration. It's not easy to ski and chat, just like it's difficult to run and carry on a conversation. My mind is mostly clear. I think about where to ski, I watch for thin ice and other potential dangers, and I check to make sure the others in the expedition are also doing well, that no one is falling down or lagging behind. We all watch out for one another.

We ski in a line, though sometimes one of us will go ahead of the others to look for any potential problems like thin ice or large pressure ridges that we'll need to ski around. We take breaks for food, for the bathroom, and to rest. We stop to sleep, but it really doesn't matter when because there is no darkness during this time of year. In the spring and summer up in the north, there is twenty-four hours of daylight. In the winter, it's the opposite—twenty-four hours of darkness. Later in the day the sun dips lower to the horizon, but it never actually sets. It's just an object in the sky. I don't actually feel any warmth from the sun.

Our team stops and pitches our tents in the ice, preparing for six hours of rest on our first "night" of the journey. Even though it's light out, after skiing for eighteen hours, I find it's easy to collapse into a deep sleep. As soon as we wake up, we pack up our camp for another day of travel. On an average day, we travel about fifteen miles. Moving along the ice floes isn't like traveling on land. Floes are sheets of floating ice, and the ground is always shifting. The forceful wind and current are constantly coming from the northeast. Danger is present throughout the day.

I keep focused. Because the land around me looks the same all of the time, it's easy to let my mind wander. But a wrong step can be a disaster for me and my team. To concentrate I do simple things, like focus on my breathing. I visualize where I'm going, and I remember my purpose—to ski to the North Pole. I must

keep warm, but I can't sweat too much or it could freeze on me. Every day I push my body to its limit.

The days turn to weeks and the sun climbs higher in the sky—each day brings us closer to the summer solstice. It's April 26 now. It's getting warmer, too. I find that –13 Fahrenheit (–25 degrees Celsius) is a good temperature for me. Anything warmer than that makes me uncomfortable because my clothes are designed for extreme cold. Warmer temperatures also mean more open water and faster drifting ice.

The warm weather makes travel more dangerous. As I ski along, I notice the ice is getting thin—it's now maybe an inch to an inch and a half thick. It sinks under my weight about five or six inches as I travel over it—it's like skiing on a trampoline. I yell to the rest of the team, "Do not stop!" If any of us stops on ice this thin, we could easily fall through. The trick is to glide quickly and lightly.

We soon discover that when we wake up each day, we are about three miles behind where we were when we went to sleep. The ice moves at such a fast rate that it's like traveling on a giant conveyer belt moving backward. It's frustrating to lose ground while we sleep, but the movement also keeps us determined on our journey. We can never rest too long or take any days off because it's just more distance we will have to cover later.

Each day looks like the one before it. Ice, snow, sun—the landscape doesn't change much. But as the weather warms up in May, the ice moves even faster and there is more open water. I always have to pay attention no matter how tired I get.

When we find open water, we sometimes need to figure out a way to get across. In some spots, we go way to the left or right to ski around the open water.

Angus leading the team

Other times we make our own bridge with floating ice. We push one floating sheet of ice in front of another with our hands and ski poles and then move quickly across these small, frozen islands. Keeping balance is critical when skiing across a floating piece of ice. We go one person at a time and keep our weight in the middle.

It's May 14 and the team is about five miles away from the North Pole. We're so close to our final destination. I'm tired and excited, but also thinking about getting back home to my family. I think about how much I've changed during this trip. I was the only person on the team without prior expedition experience, so in the beginning I was mostly following. But now, as we near the end, I feel like I've taken a leadership role. Misha Malakhov, the Russian arctic expert, and I are taking charge now. The more difficult the conditions, the more we seem to thrive and push ahead.

Five miles away and I'm leading the team. I can see that the ice is getting thinner and soft, but I keep

Five miles away and I'm leading the team.

A frosty Angus Cockney

pushing ahead. I'm energized, thinking about never having to look at a compass again or eat that awful food again . . .

. . . when one of my legs breaks through the ice! It's an absolutely frightening moment. I have close to sixty pounds of supplies on my back. I may be athletic and agile, but if I go completely through the ice here, I won't make it. The icy water would swallow me. For all my experience now in extreme conditions, I am terrified. I shout out to the rest of the team. They stop and gather in together like they're trying to figure out a plan. But seven people cannot rush toward a spot where the ice is breaking or everyone will be lost.

I push my poles into the snow around me, arch my back, and slide my leg and ski out from the icy water. Pulling myself out of the hole in the ice, I feel very lucky to be able to get out on my own. It's cold, but my waterproof boots and pants have protected me. I'm okay. This mishap was a warning to the team and me not to lose focus. Even though we're near the end, there's still danger.

I move away quickly from the hole where I fell and I get straight back to my task. I keep heading north, leading the team forward. More ice, more snow, and more sun. Just five more miles. When we finally reach the North Pole, we know we're here only because our instruments and compass tell us so. There's no clear marking. Traveling to the North Pole is not like climbing a mountain where you know you're at the top when you can't climb any higher.

I'm excited to reach our goal, but I also feel it's kind of a letdown. We've reached the North Pole and there's nothing here but more ice and more snow. After taking it all in, we radio a message to the people at our base camp and they send out airplanes to come pick us up. We carve out a landing strip in the ice for the plane to land and take off. And then we wait. The plane arrives and we all board it, exhausted.

The flight back takes only four hours. It's amazing that it took us fifty-six days to walk to the North Pole from base camp but such a short time to go back by plane.

On the flight back, I think about what incredible things the human body can do. We can adapt to any kind of environment on earth and push through extreme conditions. The survival instinct is so strong. So is the motivation to achieve. I set my goal, I was committed, and I reached the North Pole! It's a memory I will take with me for the rest of my life. No matter what adversity I may face in the future, I know I can conquer anything after this.

The Icewalk was a one-time expedition put together by Robert Swan. Three years prior, Swan had led a group walk to the South Pole in Antarctica. The Icewalk was his attempt to be the first man to reach both poles by foot. The team filmed the journey to help raise awareness about the importance of protecting the environment and preserving the Arctic. Today **ANGUS COCKNEY** lives in Alberta, Canada, where he is an artist and speaker.

WHAT IT'S LIKE...
To Run Your First Marathon...

NAME: Dean Karnazes
DATE: 1976
LOCATION: San Clemente,
California

I'm fourteen years old and a high school freshman, and our school is having a fund-raiser to benefit local underprivileged children. Participating students have asked friends, family, and neighbors to sponsor us for each lap that we can run around the high school track. Most people pledge a dollar per lap. Four laps around is one mile.

It's a big, school-wide fund-raiser. The band is playing in the field, there are food stalls along the track, and people are cheering—it's a big deal. The run begins after school one day, and after ten laps or so, some of the kids start to peel away. Once we get to lap thirty, the crowd is getting thin. Only a few of us are running now, but I still feel okay. By lap forty, 10 miles in, the few remaining runners can't believe I'm still going. I start to wonder if I could do an entire marathon—26.2 miles. What would happen to my body? Would I hallucinate? Would my legs blow apart? Would I pass out?

I ignore those thoughts and keep running around and around the track. The sun is setting now, and I'm the last one running. The only people left are some of my best friends who are cheering, waiting to see just how far I will go. After 105 laps—26.25 miles—I stop. My friends form a circle around me and are yelling and slapping my back. It's a great celebration. The next day, with sore legs and missing toenails, I walk around my neighborhood and feel like a champ. I now know I'm capable of running a marathon. It feels great. I knock on people's doors and say, "Thanks for pledging a dollar per lap. You owe me $105."

"Thanks for pledging a dollar per lap. You owe me $105."

Of course, that was not the end of my running. After years of doing marathons and ultramarathons—which is any race that is more than 26.2 miles—I decide to attempt my greatest running challenge to date.

. . . and Run Fifty Marathons in Fifty States in Fifty Consecutive Days

NAME: Dean Karnazes
DATES: September 17–November 5, 2006
LOCATION: United States of America

I'm in St. Charles, Missouri, for the Lewis and Clark Marathon. This is the two hundredth anniversary of the explorers Lewis and Clark's journey to the West Coast. It's a fitting place to begin fifty days of marathon running. I'm really nervous at the start, but more than anything, I have hope that I can get this race done. The outcome of running a marathon is always uncertain. You're never guaranteed to finish, and that's what I love about it.

Thankfully I'm not alone in this challenge. Various friends have decided to join me in a few races, and I have my team—which includes my driver, videographers (who are making a documentary), photographers, and tour manager—supporting me the whole way. Some of the marathons are organized, and some have to be put together by my team. For the races we've put together, official judges need to be brought in.

The race begins. Starting in the right way is important. I'm well hydrated and mentally ready. The beginning of the race is mostly flat roads. The trick is not to start too fast. After experimenting with speed in the first few miles, I find a comfortable pace that should put me across the finish line in under four hours.

There are so many thoughts going through my mind during the race. Sometimes I think about practical things: *Are my shoes tight? Are my socks*

pulled up? Then there are moments when I'm floating along in the "zone." This is the best part of the run because my mind is clear—I'm like a running machine and every step feels good.

The race continues and the miles seem to tick away, but then there are moments of pain. My quads and calves are burning. The pain comes and goes in cycles until I reach twenty miles: this is the infamous "wall." It's physical, but mostly mental. All long-distance runners go through it. I struggle to get past the idea that I can't finish. Some of the steps hurt. I slow my pace just a bit to collect my thoughts before shaking off the doubt and pain. I know I can finish.

I finish the Lewis and Clark Marathon in three hours, fifty minutes, and fifty-two seconds. As soon as I'm done, I have events to go to: book signings, meet-and-greets, and media interviews. People know my background in running long distances from my first book, *Ultramarathon Man*. My sponsors and my team have alerted the media to my fifty-state marathon challenge.

It's dinnertime. I grab a quick bite to eat, and we drive to Memphis, Tennessee, where the next race is. During the ride, I think about how a marathon is a level playing field. I start the marathon as an equal to every other runner. Those people standing next to me are my brothers and sisters. Even professional runners know that at some point the marathon is going to break them down. When that happens to my fellow runner, this person I've been battling with, I turn to him and help him through his struggles. I know the same thing will happen to me, and I'm going to need help picking up the pieces, too.

We get to the hotel close to midnight, and I have to recharge for the next day.

The days are exhausting, but are becoming routine. I wake up still tired, eat, and get to the race. The eighteenth day is in Hawaii—the Maui Marathon. The weather is hot and humid, making my pace a little slower than usual. I finish the race in just under four hours and twenty-seven minutes. That night I take a late flight from Hawaii to Phoenix, Arizona. I don't get much sleep on the plane, and I don't arrive at the hotel until well after midnight. I need to be awake by dawn, have my breakfast by 6:30, and get to the race for the 8 A.M. start.

Day nineteen is hot. I'm running in 103-degree Fahrenheit heat (39 degrees Celsius) on what's known as an out-and-back course—I've run this type of race before, but not in weather this hot. This means I have to run 13.1 miles out on a road, and then turn around and run back along the same route to finish. This road is so flat and so straight ahead that from the starting line I can almost see the orange turnaround cone 13.1 miles in the distance. Running this race is like experiencing some kind of horror movie. With every step forward, that turnaround point seems to get farther and farther away. I can't seem to get to that cone.

Finally, I do get there, and I almost pass out. I'm hallucinating, I'm seeing mirages in the desert, and heat waves are coming up off the asphalt. I don't have my usual mental sharpness; I feel like I'm falling apart, and the race is only half over. If I hadn't once run the Badwater Ultra Marathon—a 135-mile race that takes place in Death Valley in July, where temperatures can soar to 130 degrees Fahrenheit (54 degrees Celsius)—I wouldn't think it's possible for a human to run in conditions like these. Knowing I've been through worse helps

> Once I make the shift to that positive thinking, I know I'm going to give it everything I've got.

me get through this race. Still, I struggle back to the finish line and complete the marathon in just over four hours and forty-five minutes.

At this point in my series of races I have a lot of self-doubt, but I remind myself that I trained as hard as I could. I'm as ready for this as I can be. I just let go of any negative thoughts and say to myself, *Okay, just do the best you can when you get to the starting line every morning. You are going to be hurting, and a lot of these races are going to be tough. But make a commitment that you'll try, you'll work hard, and you'll run the best you can that day.* Once I make the shift to that positive thinking, I know I'm going to give it everything I've got. And if I fail, I will fail spectacularly.

On day twenty-one, in St. George, Utah, I run with more than 5,000 other runners and finish in just over three hours and twenty minutes. In Dallas, Texas, 75 other runners participate in the Dallas White Rock Marathon that my team has put together. I finish in just over four hours and twelve minutes. Day twenty-eight brings me to a race in Hartford, Connecticut, with more than 7,600 other marathoners. I finish in just under three hours and thirty minutes.

On day forty-one—the Atlanta, Georgia, marathon—I suffer the worst running fall of my life. With only fifty of us racing through the rain on busy streets, we are forced to stay as close to the side of the road as possible. Six miles into the race, while running past a construction site, I trip on a rusty piece of

Dean Karnazes finishing his fifty-state marathon challenge in New York City

metal sticking into the path. I fall so quickly that there's no time to put my hands out to catch myself. I land on my right forearm. I feel numbness in my right hand and I'm concerned that I broke my arm. Other runners offer to call an ambulance, but I keep running. I finish in four hours and eight minutes. There's an ambulance waiting at the finish line to tend to the deep cut in my forearm. I don't have time to go to the hospital. Besides, my legs still work. I'm ready to keep moving.

The fiftieth and last race of this challenge is the New York City Marathon. The weather is cool, around 45 degrees Fahrenheit (7 degrees Celsius). It's perfect running weather.

Though I should be exhausted, having run my heart out for the past forty-nine days, I feel strong and ready for this last marathon. When the starting gun fires, I'm off at a fast pace and feeling good. It's odd, but I keep thinking about what will come after this race. I'm not thinking about the interviews and celebrations, but my next run. The New York City Marathon is a great one for

Dean and his team celebrate the last of the fifty marathons.

me and a perfect way to end my challenge. Crossing the finish line, I record my fastest time of all fifty marathons: three hours and thirty seconds. I definitely feel a sense of accomplishment, but it's also a big letdown having finished all the races. For me, the beauty and excitement is in the journey, not the destination. In the last fifty days, I've been in all fifty states, and though I've really only seen about 26.2 miles of each of those states on this trip, I got an amazing taste of

No one bought me a plane ticket for a flight back to my home in San Francisco. So I figure I might as well run.

America. Once I cross the finish line in New York, it's just over. I had an incredible ride, and I do feel good, but all I can think about now is, *What comes next? When and where will I run again?*

The next day is full of interviews with reporters and television shows. They all want to know about my fifty races in fifty states in fifty days. I joke with some of them that my next challenge is to explore fifty couches in fifty states, but the reality is that I want to start running again. At the end of the day, I realize that there has been a bit of an oversight in the planning of my trip. No one bought me a plane ticket for a flight back to my home in San Francisco. So I figure I might as well run.

From New York City, I run all day and night before I take my first rest. In the coming days I average more than forty miles of running per day. About three weeks later, I cross the Mississippi River and find myself back in St. Charles, Missouri, where I ran the first marathon. More than ready to go home now, I book a flight and take a plane the rest of the way.

Men's Fitness claimed "he might just be the fittest man in the world," and *TIME Magazine* named him one of the "Top 100 Most Influential People in the World." **DEAN KARNAZES** travels all over the world to speak to youth groups about good health and nutrition. In addition to his fifty-state marathon challenge, he has completed many other tests of physical endurance, like an ultramarathon.

WHAT IT'S LIKE . . .
To Sail Through a Hurricane at Sea

NAME: Tami Oldham Ashcraft
DATES: September 22–
November 21, 1983
LOCATION: Pacific Ocean,
Tahiti to Hawaii

The offer is too good to pass up. My fiancé, Richard, and I have been hired to sail the forty-four-foot Trintella luxury yacht, Hazana, from Tahiti to San Diego, California. I'm sad to leave my friends in Tahiti. Though we've been here only a few months, we quickly bonded with other sailors and some of the locals. But San Diego is home for me. Considering both of us love being at sea, there is no way we can say no to the opportunity.

We set sail on the afternoon of September 22. Our plan is to head east as far as possible so that we can ease the sails a bit—or let some of the wind spill out—and have a slower, smoother ride north up to San Diego. That's the plan.

Three days into our trip, we discover that we are heading into a lot of strong wind and rough seas. It's hard work steering the boat, keeping our balance, and managing the massive sail. The boat pounds into the waves. One of the deck fittings that we use to tie down equipment comes loose, allowing seawater to leak into the cabin down below, where we sleep and cook our meals. Some water drips onto the single-side band radio, which we use to contact people over longer distances. This destroys the radio completely. We're not concerned, though, because we still have a little VHF radio that we use to contact ships we can see. We decide to change our direction to head toward the north, where we hope to find calmer waters. Hopefully this will ease the strain on the boat and our bodies.

We receive regular weather reports from our radio on the boat. After a week at sea, we learn that there's a tropical depression, which is a type of powerful storm, forming to the east of us. We are so far west that we don't give the storm much thought. These depressions usually move north, where they lose strength off the coast of Mexico. Besides, the storm is almost two thousand miles from where we are. There's no need to change course, and the weather is beautiful— sunny and calm. We have good wind and good seas.

It's early October now, and we hear on the radio that the tropical depression has been updated to hurricane status: Hurricane Raymond. We still don't alter our course because the storm is so far away. It should turn north if it follows its expected course.

We keep hearing more weather reports. The hurricane is growing larger and it's now heading west. We plot a route north to try to get out of the storm's way, but the days are still sunny and the seas are calm. Richard and I are not concerned.

As we begin our new course, I'm still calm, but Richard grows more worried. He's sailed in a hurricane before and knows he doesn't want to again. I've sailed through strong winds and storms. I don't think it will be a big problem if the hurricane brushes close to us.

It's October 11, and now the skies are overcast and gray. We track the storm with our radio and realize we're headed for a Category 4 hurricane. The storm is too big and moving too quickly in our direction.

The wind is now steady at twenty miles per hour, and we're trying to move as fast as possible. We now know we're not going to completely get out of this one untouched. Richard seems nervous but focused. I'm still not scared. I have faith in our boat and our abilities to sail her in rough weather.

The next day, I'm on early-morning watch on the deck of the boat. By 4 A.M., Hurricane Raymond is upon us. The seas are rough, and each wave slaps against the hull of the yacht. I can taste salt every time I breathe because the wind is whipping the seawater and rain all around me. Still, the boat is

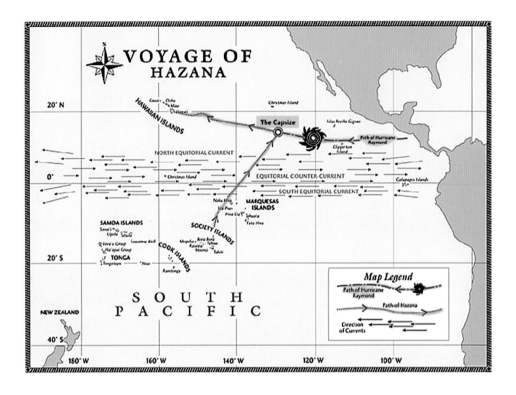

handling the storm so far. It's hard work steering, but I'm still trying to sail us north and out of the worst of Hurricane Raymond.

By 7 A.M., the winds are getting much worse. Richard isn't able to sleep or even rest anymore because of the pounding the boat is taking. He comes up to help me.

By 9 A.M., the wind is intense, and the seas are swelling. We take down the sails completely—down to what we call bare-pole—and run the boat's motor to try to keep moving forward through the rough seas. We know we're going to have to ride this one out. All we can do is point the bow, or front part of the boat,

at the oncoming waves so that we don't roll over.

Now I'm scared—this is the worst weather I've ever seen. The wind is just howling. I've never heard wind howling like that. It sounds like it's whistling through the mast, wires, and ropes. The sound grows until it's a constant roar, like jet engines. This goes on for hours. I'm anxious. The rain feels like pellets hitting my skin. It hurts. Richard and I duck behind the windscreen on the front of the cockpit for shelter.

Richard is now steering through waves that are fifty feet tall! We're in the worst of it. As the boat comes up over these huge waves, his body is lifted right off the deck. Thankfully he is holding on tight to the wheel; otherwise he'd go overboard. Now we are worried about being blown off the boat, so we attach ourselves to the boat with tethers, strong straps of fabric that act as safety harnesses for ourselves. We come up over the top of one huge wave—the boat practically flies off the crest of the wave—and then we come crashing down off the backside. This happens over and over again. The sound and intensity of it all is absolutely frightening. I think this poor boat might just split in half from the force. If the boat splits, we won't survive.

Richard is now steering through waves that are fifty feet tall!

We ride out the big waves and just hold on, keeping our heads down. There's not much more we can do right now. Richard and I need to shout over the sound of the wind to communicate with each other. He suggests I go to the cabin below to try to rest. I hate to leave him at the wheel all alone but I agree. I'm not much help at this point, so I go.

In the cabin, everything is stowed well, so nothing is flying around. I sit down and try to get a weather update on the radio, but of course there's no reception in the storm. After attaching my safety harness to the leg of a table, I take off my jacket and look at the clock on the wall. It's 1 in the afternoon.

Suddenly, I hear Richard scream, "Oh my God!" At that moment, my feet come off the ground and the boat drops out from under me. I hear this big

SLAP and I try to cover my head with my arms. The boat begins to roll over as something hits my head—everything goes black.

I wake up with a start. My eyes pop open. I'm on my back and lying on the bench next to the galley table. A ton of debris is on top of me—a broken door, cushions, food, and books. I must be in the middle of a nightmare. I look up and all I can see is this big hole where the main mast of the boat had been. I see the sky. Blue sky. I push all the stuff off me so that I can sit up. The clock on the wall reads 4 P.M. I don't know where I am. I don't know anything.

When I sit up, I realize there's water up to my knees. I know I'm in big trouble, wherever I am. I suddenly remember I'm on a boat, and it must be sinking! I unhook my safety harness. The ladder that leads up to the deck is gone, so I have to climb up to get out of the cabin and to the cockpit. In the cockpit there's this tether attached to a cleat, or metal prong that is attached to the boat and used for securing ropes. The tether is hanging off the side deck, and that's when everything comes back to me—the hurricane, the fifty-foot waves,

everything. That's Richard's safety harness! I grab the line and yank, but there's nothing there. Just the bitter end. I lose it. I scream his name.

I throw anything that can float into the water, desperately trying to save Richard, wherever he is. I also do this to see which way the sea is drifting so that I can go look for him. My survival instincts kick in. I find our binoculars and look in all directions, but I don't see anything. I know Richard is gone and the tears start coming.

There are gashes on my shin and head. I'm not bleeding now, but I can tell I had been. I'm very weak and I must have lost a lot of blood. At this point, I almost start to freak out, but I quickly pull myself together. I hear this voice in my head say, *Don't leave your boat.* You learn that from the moment you start out on the water—whatever you do, do *not* leave the boat.

I inflate the tiny life raft and tie it onto the side deck. I want the raft ready in case the boat sinks and I need it to survive. I take note of the supplies I still have. I go back down to the cabin to load whatever I can into the raft. Now it's *my* survival I'm worried about. I get a good amount of food and supplies in the raft when a wave hits the boat. Everything inside the raft spills overboard and sinks.

I can't take it anymore! I'm at my wit's end. I slide into the empty raft and just lie inside, falling in and out of consciousness. I'm shaking. I don't know if I sleep or faint, but when I open my eyes again, it's morning. I crawl out of the raft and into the boat on my hands and knees. I'm so sore. After looking in the cabin below, I can tell the boat had rolled over while I was unconscious. The boat had also pitch-poled, meaning it flipped end over end during the violent storm. I must have flopped around, hanging on by that six-foot rope. Everything hurts.

I realize I have to make something—anything—happen if I want to survive. I need to get the boat moving. I try the engine and it doesn't work. Almost everything on the boat is damaged or broken—I have no radio, no stove for cooking, no running water to clean myself. But at least it's still floating. I begin to figure out what is left that works. I have a nine-foot pole and enough rope to put together a temporary mast, and I drape a small sail over it. It's not big, and it's not perfect, but it gets the boat moving! This gives me hope that I might survive.

A sextant, which is a navigation device

I look over the ocean charts and realize that my only option, given the wind and the ocean currents, is to head northwest and catch the Pacific current to the Hawaiian islands. I know my trip will take weeks. If I miss the Hawaiian islands, I won't have enough food or water to make it to Asia. Hawaii or rescue is my only chance.

It's mid-October and I'm floating through the Pacific Ocean. I'm surviving on small sips of water from the emergency supplies and a little food here and there. I'm taking navigation readings with my sextant, a tool that sailors have used for hundreds of years. By lining up the horizon with the position of the sun and checking the readings against the date and time in a book, I can figure out my exact position on the ocean. Using mathematical formulas, I can navigate. I have some control now. Taking these navigational readings is keeping me sane as the days turn to weeks. I've figured out I'm covering between twenty to sixty miles per day. Cleaning the boat also helps keep me sane.

I'm losing weight from eating so little, but I'm still able to keep myself alive. It's late October when I work to break into the boat's water tank and discover that I have twenty-five gallons of drinkable water. This is a huge turning point—I know I have enough water now. I'm able to survive.

In early November, I see a ship on the horizon. I can't believe what I'm seeing, but it's there! I pull out a flare gun and fire flares into the air—I'm desperate to be seen. I tie a red shirt to an oar and wave it back and forth. I fire another flare. But the ship doesn't change course. It never sees me. I realize then how far away the ship is. I don't have much of a chance.

A week later I see another ship. This one is much closer. I fire off a bunch of flares to make myself seen. I even set off parachute flares—they shoot high into the air and fall back down on a parachute, so they burn for a long time. The ship looks like it's coming toward me and I'm sure the crew sees me. But the boat keeps on going by until it disappears from view. This time I'm more upset than I was before. The boat was so close. I'm devastated. I start to think the boat was some kind of dream.

It's mid-November when I start to see signs that I'm getting closer to land, like

I see a ship on the horizon. I can't believe what I'm seeing, but it's there!

floating soda bottles. Then I see a low-flying military aircraft. I scurry for the
flare gun once again and fire more flares into the sky. Seeing the plane also
means I'm getting closer to land. A plane like that wouldn't have the fuel to travel
across the ocean. I fire more flares, but the plane keeps on flying. No dip of the
wing to acknowledge me. Nothing. Now I'm at the tail end of my exhaustion and
I'm starting to lose hope. I've survived for weeks already, but this is the third
time I thought I would be rescued and the third time I wasn't seen.

The *Hazana* in port after the storm

It's November 21 around 2:30 in the morning. I'm sitting in the cockpit and keeping my watch. I'm delirious with exhaustion, but I see something on the horizon. There are lights—colored lights. It's not a ship—it's land!

I check my charts and realize I'm near the harbor of Hilo, Hawaii. I've been alone at sea for forty-one days and land is just ahead of me. I want so badly to pull the boat into harbor right now and get on shore, but I know I can't sail through the reefs and harbor at night—especially without a navigation chart. I've come too far to sink on a shallow reef now. I'm forced to sit until morning.

As day breaks, I see a large ship coming out of the harbor. Again I fire a flare. This time the ship stops. The crew sees me! The captain calls the Coast Guard

Tami Oldham Ashcraft, the day after her rescue

to tow me in to shore. I have an incredible sense of relief that my sea voyage is over as the Coast Guard boat comes to rescue me. But the relief comes with a realization: life is so fragile. This experience has really taught me how strong I am—I was able to cling to life with all my strength and use any means to keep myself alive. I know I will keep moving forward. I will sail again. I owe it to myself and to Richard.

TAMI OLDHAM ASHCRAFT wrote a book called *Red Sky in Mourning: A True Story of Love, Loss, and Survival at Sea* about her weeks lost on the ocean. She currently lives in Washington with her family and is still an avid sailor.

WHAT IT'S LIKE . . .
To Lose Both of Your Legs to Frostbite . . .

NAME: Mark Inglis
DATES: November 16–29, 1982
LOCATION: Mount Cook,
New Zealand

I'm in charge of one of two search-and-rescue teams on Mount Cook in New Zealand. I'm doing a practice climb on the east ridge of Mount Cook, which is quite a significant ice climb on the tallest mountain in the country. We have a new team member, Phil, and we all need to learn to work together. If you're going to jump out of a helicopter at twelve thousand feet, rescue someone, and put yourself in a pretty dangerous situation, you need to know the person you're jumping out with. The best way to do that is to go climbing together.

Phil and I reach the east ridge of Mount Cook and see there are clouds rolling in. Snow is starting to fall, but it's not that bad. I've seen worse on this mountain. But soon, the weather is much worse. Suddenly the wind and snow have picked up and the conditions are turning bad.

We're too far from the base to turn around. Once we come across the top of Mount Cook, however, we realize how bad our situation is. The storm continues to get worse. We can't see more than a few feet in front of us, and the temperature is dropping. We have to find a place to protect ourselves because the wind and cold could kill you in the mountains. I know there's a small cave near the summit of the mountain, so we sneak in there.

The ice cave has about as much space as you'd have under an office desk. There's not enough room to lie down or even sit up—just enough space to huddle together. We have some food with us: half a packet of biscuits, a small tin of peaches, a container of energy drink powder, and a chocolate bar. We have only the clothes on our back, our climbing gear, and not much else because we weren't planning on an overnight trip. We don't have a radio, but our other team members are expecting us. Given the storm, it won't take them long to realize we're in trouble.

This is a unique situation—I'm going to have to be saved by my own search-and-rescue team. Perhaps if I didn't know them all so well, I would lose hope. But I have incredible faith in my team, and they know that we are doing the right things up here in order to survive. We stay close to keep warm, conserve our food, and keep inside the small cave. We don't want to risk facing the weather and getting lost without any shelter nearby.

After two days in the cave, the weather is showing no sign of letting up.

Each day we venture out to see if we can attempt to climb down, but the storm is too strong. We're stuck. Around the third day

This is a unique situation—I'm going to have to be saved by my own search-and-rescue team.

I start to get frostbite in my feet—they feel numb, and I can see that they look really pale. They're starting to freeze. I feel weak, but still I venture out to see if there's enough of a break in the weather to attempt a rescue. No luck.

Each day we shiver. We try to rub our arms and legs to keep the blood flowing, but we don't talk too much. We have little food, so we can't use up too many calories. Each day drags. I try to sleep as much as possible, but it's difficult being in such a cramped space, hungry, and so cold. Each day I expect the storm to end, but it doesn't.

By day five, our food is gone, and my feet are pretty much completely frozen. I can't feel them. I've lost too much weight and am too weak to stand to go outside. Never in the history of New Zealand has a storm lasted so long. On day seven, we receive a bag dropped from a helicopter that contains food and high-calorie fluids for drinking. But the weather is so bad that the helicopter can't land to rescue us, and we're too weak to move anyway. Rescuers will have to come carry us out.

It's not until the fourteenth day, November 29, 1982, that there's a break in the weather. The ground crew finally comes to rescue us.

I'm so relieved to hear them calling out to us as they get close. I know we're going to survive. However, I'm also afraid for their safety. I want to be rescued, of course, but I don't want others to be hurt or killed in the process. I care about my team a great deal.

My team arrives and straps me to a plastic stretcher. Next, they strap in Phil and drag us down the mountain to a point where we can be loaded onto a helicopter.

I arrive at the hospital that day. The doctors tell me I've lost 40 percent of my body weight. But still I think, *I'll be here for another two weeks; I might lose a few toes to frostbite, and then be out of here*. I find out the frostbite is much worse than that. They have to amputate both of my legs at the knees. There is no choice in the matter. If my legs aren't removed, I could die.

I'm really frustrated when I get my new artificial legs. I can't do simple things, like walking or climbing stairs, as well as I did before. I'm upset that I won't be able to climb mountains like I used to. I know I don't have a choice. I need to find something else to do. It's not just about learning to walk, run, and climb; I have to learn to think differently. I think about how life is—about the opportunities it offers and not about the problems it throws your way.

I go back to Mount Cook and work there for another couple of years, but realize that I can't do this climbing thing as well as I could before. I move on to other jobs. I become a research scientist, then a winemaker, but I never forget about mountain climbing. A longing for the mountains has always been in my blood. But I don't want people to help me up the mountain—I want to do it myself.

It takes years, but I start to figure out how to climb with my artificial legs. And every mountain climber knows the challenge of Mount Everest is always calling. I am determined to climb the mountain, and in 2006 I do.

. . . and Climb Mount Everest—the World's Tallest Mountain

NAME: Mark Inglis
DATES: March 25–
  May 25, 2006
LOCATION: Mount Everest, Tibet

My climbing team and I are heading toward Mount Everest, driving across a Tibetan plateau at an altitude higher than the highest mountain in New Zealand. We cross a place called Pang La Pass, and straight ahead about fifty miles away is the north side of Mount Everest. A big plume of wind is coming off the top of it, billowing snow and clouds. I think, *How on earth am I going to get up there?*

The climbing team goes silent. We're all awestruck in the presence of this monster of a mountain. I finally realize the size of the dream, the project, whatever it is that I've put in front of myself. The mountain is both an incredibly inspiring and frightening sight.

We arrive at base camp, and I think about my strategy for climbing Mount Everest. The camp looks like a big, dry riverbed at the end of a glacier. It's windy. Dust and yak feces kick up and fly around. I find myself needing to wear a mask because of all the debris. You can see the summit from anywhere in the camp. It's quite intimidating.

I spend about two weeks at base camp adjusting to the altitude, which is about eighteen thousand feet. At this height, you have half the available

Mark Inglis at Advanced Base Camp

oxygen that's at sea level. Up here you can take only every second breath. It's like having asthma.

Every two days, we make a climb. The point of these practice climbs is to get my body used to working in high altitude and with little oxygen. I don't need many supplies for these climbs, just some water and food, my ropes, and a pack. In some places we're hiking on ice, and in others we're scaling rock and ice walls to pull ourselves up the mountain. The team and I climb up between five hundred and one thousand feet or so, then climb back down to base camp and recover for two days. Because there's so little oxygen up here, it takes days to recover from a climb that would be pretty easy at sea level. To climb Mount Everest, you need to be healthy and strong. Also, allowing time to recover is important. Those who don't reach the top often don't make it because they didn't give themselves enough time to recover properly.

After two weeks of practice climbs, we begin the nearly fourteen-mile climb to Advanced Base Camp, which is about twenty-one thousand feet above sea level. It takes us two days to get there by walking up the glacier. Those two days are so tough. I feel each step I take in every muscle.

Staying at Advanced Base Camp is hard, because it sits so high above sea level, just underneath the part of the mountain called the North Col—a pass leading up the north side of Mount Everest. Staying here makes me feel like I have the flu all the time. I'm nauseous, I want to vomit, my head spins, I feel dizzy, and it's really hard to sleep at night. During the day I stay

in my little tent, just breathing. It's about 85 degrees Fahrenheit (29 degrees Celsius) in the tent because of the sun's radiation. The minute the sun goes down, the temperature immediately drops to 5 degrees Fahrenheit (-15 degrees Celsius). I really start to appreciate a good sleeping bag at Advanced Base Camp.

Just like at base camp, I do a five-hundred- to one-thousand-foot climb every few days, and then come back down to recover. On some climbs I spend the night in my tent on the North Col. On others I go up and come down the same day.

During one descent I get into some trouble. I'm coming down an ice cliff, and on the way the rope breaks, sending me tumbling. I come to a stop in a pile of snow and look beside me. One of my artificial legs is broken in two. Thankfully I can just pull a roll of duct tape out of my pack, tape up my leg, and limp down. When I get back to Advanced Base Camp, I rebuild my leg using extra parts I brought with me.

After three weeks at Advanced Base Camp, we start to look for a break in the weather to attempt the summit. During most years there are only about thirty days when you can get to the top of Mount Everest. Otherwise the weather is so bad that you can't survive. The timing needs to be just right. We've found out the next few days are supposed to be good, so we start our summit climb from Advanced Base Camp.

We head up the north ridge to Camp One, then on to Camp Two, to Camp Three, and finally to Camp Four, which sits at around 27,200 feet above sea level. At each camp, breathing is harder. Each step is more difficult than the last. We spend less than a day at each camp. We rest to recover so that we can continue the climb. By Camp Three, I need to start using oxygen. A person can carry only so much oxygen in a tank, so now, to attempt the summit, the timing is critical.

Mark at the summit of Mount Everest

The area around Camp Four is an incredibly tough place to be. You go past bodies of climbers who died on the mountain. When I see them, I make a pact with myself: *That will not be me.* I realize that a lot of the problems happen on the way back down. The goal of climbing Mount Everest is to stand on the summit. That's fantastic, but it's only halfway. If you don't have enough energy left after you get to the summit, you won't make it down alive.

On May 15, 2006, we get the word that the weather is going to get worse in the coming days. If we want to attempt the summit, we have to go now. We continue to climb from Camp Four, faster now and with our goal in mind. The weather is very, very cold—about –60 degrees Fahrenheit (-51 degrees Celsius). I can't stop moving for more than thirty seconds because I will start to get too cold and risk getting frostbite again. I have to keep moving to keep my heart rate up and my blood flowing. That day is very tough.

There's an area on the north side of Mount Everest called the Second Step. It's a very difficult bit of rock climbing. It's just above twenty-eight thousand feet, and it takes me three tries to climb up to where I can hike again. Once I'm above the Second Step, I realize that this is where Mount Everest goes from being a physical challenge to a mental challenge. It's a mental challenge in two ways. The mountain questions your training and skill. *Are you tough enough*

to keep going? the mountain seems to ask. The other mental challenge is that it threatens your powers of reasoning. Are you smart enough to know when to turn around in order to survive?

The last part of the climb up the north ridge to the summit is slow and tough. Though it's not very steep up here, the wind whips at me over the mountain peak. Exposed rock, snow, and ice lie ahead. I need to concentrate on every step so that I don't make a mistake now that I'm so close. I keep my head down and will each leg to move. I take five steps, then fifteen breaths, five steps, then fifteen breaths. . . .

The only reason I know I've reached the top is because there are no more steps to take. It's 7 A.M., and I finally look up. I am standing at the top of Mount Everest!

I look out at the horizon and I can see the curvature of the earth. The mountains below me all look tiny. I can see cloud banks far below me that surround the smaller mountains. I can see several countries from here—China, Nepal, Bangladesh, and India. The summit is very small. It's just a snowy area where only a couple of people can stand at one time. An incredible wave of relief comes over me—I've done it! But immediately I feel an equally large wave of nervousness and fear. I realize I'm only halfway to reaching my goal. I still have to get back down.

For a double amputee, going down is fifteen times harder than climbing up. My artificial legs are built to go on flat surfaces or uphill.

Are you tough enough to keep going? the mountain seems to ask.

When I walk downhill, the impact on the stumps of my legs is very painful. I realize I'm the first double amputee to have reached the summit of Mount Everest, but it only matters if I make it back.

From the moment I stand on the summit, I have only one picture in my mind: my family. That's what helps me get through the whole climb down. Descending Mount Everest is like wading into a soup of oxygen. It's fantastic. With every step farther down the mountain, strength just flows through me. The climb becomes easier with every step. Once I get back down to Camp Four, I call my family, because from here I know I can survive. Getting off the phone, I realize I've finally accomplished what I've wanted to for so long. It feels amazing to have done this.

People ask me now, "You've climbed Mount Everest; what more is there to do?" For me, there are just so many opportunities. My biggest challenge now is trying to decide on my next Everest-like accomplishment.

MARK INGLIS still climbs mountains and is an active adventurer and motivational speaker. He lives in New Zealand with his family.

Acknowledgments

First, I must thank everyone who shared their deeply personal and profound stories with me. Every conversation changed my life in some way, and for that I'm grateful. Thanks to Brooke Dworkin for helping get this idea off the ground, and thank you to Alli Brydon for all of your editorial work and for seeing this through to completion. Thanks also to Stacey Perry for transposing most of these interviews. My wife and my daughter also have my gratitude for putting up with me and believing in me when I needed a little support. No one is ever in the fight alone.

Photo Credits

© Clifford White/CORBIS: viii, 3

© Kirk Aeder/IconSMI/CORBIS: 5, 6

© Frank Trapper/CORBIS: 7

© Galen Rowell/CORBIS: 80

© Reuters/CORBIS: front cover (top right)

© Marbo / Dreamstime.com: 8

© Richard Kelly / Dreamstime.com: 25

© Scott McPartland/StormStock: 47 (right)

Courtesy of U.S. Air Force: 58, 59 (bottom)

Courtesy of U.S. Air Force photo/Staff Sgt. Kristi Machado: 50

Courtesy of U.S. Air Force photo/Master Sgt. Scott Reed: 52 (top)

Courtesy of U.S. Air Force photo/Tech. Sgt. Justin D. Pyle: 52 (bottom), 56

Courtesy of U.S. Air Force photo/Tech. Sgt. Larry A. Simmons: back cover (flap), 53

Courtesy of U.S. Air Force photo/Tom Randle: 54

Courtesy of U.S. Air Force photo/Tech. Sgt. Shane A. Cuomo: 57

Courtesy of U.S. Air Force photo/Tech. Sgt. Raheem Moore: 59 (top)

© iStockphoto.com / Dean Turner: front cover (bottom) and back cover, vi–vii

© iStockphoto.com / Anthony Seebaran: 11

© iStockphoto.com / Bryan Myhr: 14

© iStockphoto.com / Duncan Noakes: 20

© iStockphoto.com / Marco Coda: 26

© iStockphoto.com / Clint Spencer: 42

© iStockphoto.com / David Parsons: 72, 130

© iStockphoto.com / Justin Grover: 76

© iStockphoto.com / Tomasz Resiak: 85

© iStockphoto.com / Felix Möckel: 102

© iStockphoto.com / Jens Carsten Rosemann: 108

© iStockphoto.com / hoyaboy: 111

© iStockphoto.com / Charles Schug: 113

© iStockphoto.com / Dean Turner: 116

© iStockphoto.com / Grazyna Niedzieska: 127

Photos courtesy of National Aeronautics and Space Administration (NASA): front cover (top left), i, 62, 63, 65, 68, 69, 71

Photos courtesy of Michael Anthony: 10, 16, 18

Photos courtesy of Tami Oldham Ashcraft: 105, 106, 109, 114, 115

© Rob Brooks-Bilson: 36–37

Photo courtesy of Phil Broscovak: 78

Photos courtesy of Angus Cockney: 82, 87, 88

Photos courtesy of Mark Inglis: 122, 124, 126, 129

Photos courtesy of Dean Karnazes: 90, 94, 96, 97, 99, 100

Photos courtesy of Jeff Kraft: 23

Photo by Rochelle M. Kraft: 27

Photos by Travis Lindhorst: 28, 30, 33, 35, 40

Photo courtesy of Sandra Magnus: iv, 60, 67, 70

© Steve Marr: 74

© Gene Moore: 44, 45, 46, 47 (left), 48

© Jonathan Romano: 13

Art by James Slupatchuk: 39

Photos by Scott Stewart: 22

Index